MW00387466

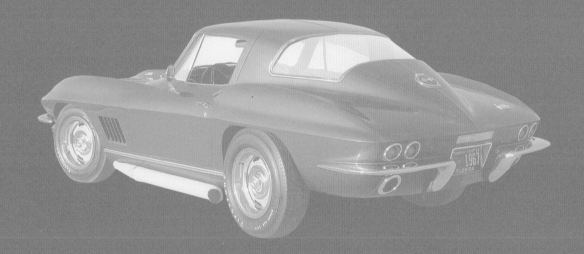

-ESSENTIAL-
MUSCLECARS

-ESSENTIAL-
MUSCLECARS

Mike Mueller

MOTORBOOKS
INTERNATIONAL

DESIGNER: Philip Clucas MSIAD
COLOUR REPRODUCTION: Berkeley Square
Printed and Bound in China

This edition published in 2004 by Motorbooks
International, an imprint of MBI Publishing
Company, Galtier Plaza, Suite 200, 380 Jackson
Street, St. Paul, MN 55101-3885 USA

© Colin Gower Enterprises Ltd.

All rights reserved. With the exception of quoting
brief passages for the purposes of review, no part of
this publication may be reproduced without prior
written permission from the Publisher.

The information in this book is true and complete
to the best of our knowledge. All recommendations
are made without any guarantee on the part of the
author or Publisher, who also disclaim any liability
incurred in connection with the use of this data or
specific details.

We recognize that some words, model names and
designations, for example, mentioned herein are
the property of the trademark holder.
We use them for identification purposes only.
This is not an official publication.

Motorbooks International titles are also available at
discounts in bulk quantity for industrial or sales-
promotional use. For details write to Special Sales
Manager at Motorbooks International Wholesalers
& Distributors, Galtier Plaza, Suite 200, 380 Jackson
Street, St. Paul, MN 55101-3885 USA.

ISBN 0-7603-1966-9

Contents

Introduction

Boss Mustang, Z/28 Camaro and Trans Am Firebird. Four-thirteen Mopar, 427 Ford, and Olds 4-4-2. Road Runner, Torino Cobra, and Hemi 'Cuda. While all these cars varied widely in size and shape, they had one thing in common—they ran like hell. Some 30 years ago we knew these high-powered haulers as "supercars." Not long before they began fading from the American scene in the early Seventies, the popular moniker became "musclecar," a name that stuck like glue and remains on the scene today.

What is a musclecar? By every definition, it's a high-performance model able to get off the line like nobody's business. Braking and handling, too, are hopefully maximized, though power has always remained the top priority. Modern musclecars, which began making their presence felt in the Eighties, do represent a nice balance of precise handling and brute force. The same, however, couldn't always be said of their forerunners, which came and went in a hurry three decades back.

By most definitions, the original musclecar era officially began in 1964 and ended roughly 10 years later. It was Pontiac that reportedly ushered in that era by introducing a ground-breaking machine that, as Car and Driver's David E. Davis, Jr., later wrote in 1975, "appeared on the American scene like a Methodist minister leaving a massage parlor." No, the legendary GTO wasn't the first American car to offer obscene amounts of horsepower. It was the way Pontiac packaged its new brand of performance that had the congregation swooning. Before the GTO came along, big cubes in big cars wearing big price tags represented the only way to fly for performance buyers. Pontiac planners then proved that less could be more. Put a big engine into a not-so-big car priced right and presto, an instant winner.

But Pontiac people weren't the first to recognize the value of a high power-to-weight ratio. Among others, Buick designers in 1936 had planted their big, powerful Roadmaster straight-eight engine into the relatively lightweight Special resulting in the Century, a model that then went on to become one of the Fifties' hottest tickets. Oldsmobile's lithe Rocket 88, armed with GM's trend-setting overhead-valve V8, appeared in 1949 and instantly became the leader of the postwar performance pack.

Fifteen years later, however, Pontiac designers redefined performance and gave it an all-new identity. Of course, their timing wasn't bad, either. As luck would have it, America's postwar "baby boom" was just starting to make its presence felt in the marketplace when the GTO arrived. Pontiac general manager Elliot "Pete" Estes had eyes; he could see that the market was ready for a mass-production factory hot rod, it was ready for the classic musclecar. GTOs then started screaming off showroom floors faster than Pontiac could build them.

What made Pontiac's pioneering performance car so appealing? "The message was straight-line speed," continued David E. Davis in his 1975 Car and Driver retro tribute. "And it felt like losing your virginity, going into combat and tasting your first beer all in about seven seconds. As for its milestone status, the '64 GTO was, in Davis' opinion, " the first Muscle Car... a violent, virile catalyst-car that set the pace and tone for five or six years of intense horsepower promotion out of Detroit city, the hallmark of a period that seemed like the culmination of all the dreams of all the enthusiasts on all the back roads in this country, but a period that in reality was nothing more than that—the period at he end of one short paragraph of automotive history."

Short indeed. A victim of both itself, as well as changing attitudes, the musclecar quickly soared in popularity, reaching its zenith in 1970, then even more quickly raced to its demise. By 1972, it was essentially all over but the shouting.

Why the quick death? For starters, the American musclecar represented an obvious paradox. Laws direct us to drive safely within established speed limits. Why, then, would we need a car capable of doubling posted limits with ease? As statistics apparently tell us, speed not only sells, it also kills.

The issue here, however, wasn't about need, it was about want. Freedom of choice is supposedly one of our unalienable rights as Americans, no? Yes, but that rights statement featured far less fine print then than it does today. No one was there to say we couldn't drive fast cars when the first GTO hit the streets in 1964. And no one then apparently cared that cars tended to burn fuel by the barrel load and foul the air with the by-products. At the time, only

Southern Californians knew about smog, right? As for gasoline supplies, they apparently were bottomless, and a gallon cost about a quarter, as it had for years.

How quickly things changed.

One year after the GTO's birth, lawmakers in Washington began addressing clean air issues. Federally mandated "smog controls" then began cramping the musclecar's style in 1968. Horsepower continued running strong for a few more years, but then tighter emissions controls began strangling the life out of the beast in the early Seventies. With the further mandated use of lower octane unleaded fuels right around the corner, automakers in 1971 were forced to make major compression concessions within their engines, effectively ending the road for high-performance V8s.

Other factors also played a part in the musclecar's quick death. Congress in 1965 also kicked off an especially vigorous investigation into automotive safety. Hearings conducted that summer by Senator Abraham Ribicoff, among other things, thrust East Coast lawyer Ralph Nader into the limelight. Tougher safety standards then followed. Insurance companies, too, got tough, and premiums immediately started skyrocketing. Even if the musclecar had somehow survived into the Seventies, most average buyers would've never been able to afford them.

Nor would they have been able to keep them running after the arrival of an "energy crisis" fueled by the Arab oil embargo of October 1973. Hit hard where it hurts most—in the wallet— American car buyers quickly came to grips with a newfound need to own fuel-efficient cars. This need grew so fast that the fuel-hungry musclecar all but vanished overnight with nary a whimper, as did the demand for such "gas hogs."

America's original musclecar breed was all but extinct by 1975. Mighty lean years then followed until Detroit's engineering fraternity finally developed the technology to effectively combine fuel efficiency, low contaminant counts and horsepower. The breed was then reborn.

How long it survives this second time around is anyone's guess.

Detroit's horsepower race heats up

Ask any car nut born after, say, 1946 when history's first musclecar came into this world and the answer will probably be 1964. Ah, but history goes back a long way, at least a few years before those baby boomers began loading up their diapers. As for harnessing horsepower, Detroit was busy doing that more than a few decades before Pontiac people copped those three little letters from Ferrari.

Ask anyone who wasn't just born yesterday when the first real musclecar was born and you'll get a couple different answers, none of them "GTO."

General Motors deserves credit for kick-starting Detroit's postwar horsepower race after introducing its high-winding, short-stroke overhead-valve V8 in 1949. Many old-timers look to Oldsmobile's new Rocket 88 that year as the GTO's forefather. Others claim that Chrysler's 300 "letter-series" cars, introduced in 1955 did the fathering. And let's not forget Chevrolet's Corvette, which was treated to its own new OHV V8 in 1955.

High-performance cars were plentiful during the decade's second half. DeSoto's Adventure, Dodge's D-500 and Plymouth's Fury all debuted in 1956. Chevrolet and Pontiac began fuel-injecting their passenger cars in 1957, and Ford that year even bolted on a supercharger or two. Then came the American Manufacturers Association "ban" on factory racing activities in 1957, which stopped Dearborn's speed merchants in their tracks. But while Ford was following the infamous AMA edict to the letter, all rivals simply went underground. "Backdoor" engineering projects proliferated during the late-Fifties, with Pontiac being especially active in high-performance development.

From these clandestine practices came the factory "super-stocks" of the early Sixties, bad-to-the-bone beasts built to give pro racers more to work with on dragstrips and superspeedways. By 1962, every automaker—even Ford—was in the business of putting race cars on Mainstreet U.S.A. Most of these machines were never intended to actually drive on the street, but some ended up there anyway even though all represented real pains in the butt to drive in everyday situations.

It was then left to the GTO to put it all together: performance and practicality. Once Average Joe was presented with affordable muscle that he could also use each day to simply get from point A to B with no fuss or muss, the die was cast—the "modern" musclecar was off and running.

With the Sixties came high-performance's heydays

Okay, perhaps purists can argue that Pontiac's GTO wasn't America's first musclecar. But, semantics aside, the "Goat" certainly was a milestone; it did help usher in a new breed. Perhaps its safer to say that it was the first modern musclecar; that is, it brought an existing concept up to date for a new decade. Along with that, it also spawned various knock-offs that then kicked off a fierce competition in Detroit to see which factory could outdo the other with its high-performance equipment.

Hot on the Goat's heels came Oldsmobile's 4-4-2, Buick's Gran Sport and Chevrolet's SS 396 Chevelle. Initially a limited-edition market test of sorts in 1965, the SS 396 blossomed the following year into a musclebound mass-market marvel. Three years later it unseated the GTO as America's best-selling musclecar. That same year, 1969, Plymouth's Road Runner came seemingly out of nowhere to claim the market's number two sales spot, pushing the reigning king from Pontiac back to third.

Chrysler Corporation had been a bit slow to offer its own modern musclecar, sticking instead with its factory super-stocks up into 1965. Then came Dodge and Plymouth's new "street Hemi" in 1966. Few performance engines ran like a Hemi and none were designed liked it. Hemi-head advantages included superior volumetric efficiency and excellent breathing characteristics. On the street, it was almost unbeatable until it faded from the scene in 1971, along with all of Detroit's other big-block bullies.

Ford, too, at first lagged behind, then caught up with a vengeance in April 1968 after introducing its 428 Cobra Jet V8. About the same time, Semon "Bunkie" Knudsen came on board in Dearborn, and Blue-Oval muscle developed to frightening levels during his short tenure. By 1970, however, Henry Ford II no longer cared about fast cars and winning races, and Ford's performance development all but disappeared overnight.

So too did the modern musclecar, the first modern musclecar, that is. With high-performance again on the upswing, we're now forced to define which era we're talking about. After all, what "modern" meant in 1964 and what it means in 2004 are two different things... Semantics again.

The Ponycar Performance Tale

One size didn't fit all as far as the great American musclecar was concerned. When the Sixties began it was full-sized flyers or nothing at all. But by decade's end high-performance cars were roaring off assembly lines in various forms, including even compacts.

Most prominent at the lower end of the scale were the "ponycars," named in honor of the downsized machine that originated the breed in 1964, Ford's Mustang. Few at the time noticed that Plymouth's Barracuda actually beat Ford's mass-market marvel out of the gates in the "long-hood/short-deck" sweepstakes by a few weeks, but "predator-fish-car" didn't have near the same ring anyway.

Additional rivals then followed up from General Motors in 1967: Chevrolet's Camaro and Pontiac's Firebird. New that year as well was the Mustang's corporate cousin from Mercury, the Cougar. American Motors Javelin appeared in 1968, and the lineup was completed with Chrysler Corporation's new E-body line, home to Dodge's all-new Challenger and Plymouth's redesigned 'Cuda, in 1970.

Lightweight and sporty-looking, all of these ponycars represented perfect starting points for building a new breed of factory hot rod, a plain fact not one of Detroit's movers and shakers overlooked. From AMX to Z/28, the performance ponycars were every bit as much fun as their larger rivals. And some were downright "boss."

American muscle peaks in 1970

The Sixties were a time of fast-thinking around Detroit as every automaker, including one not in Detroit (American Motors), was kept busy trying to beat the rest with the hottest performance machines on the market. Four-hundred-horsepower engines, flashy paint and graphics, heavy-duty parts lists as long as your arm—by decade's end the escalation was off and running like it would never come back down. But it did.

Arguably the zenith arrived in 1970, the year Chevrolet unleashed its 450-horse LS-6 454, the highest rated engine ever bolted together at the time. Rivals like Buick's Stage 1 455, Chrysler Corporation's 426 Hemi, and Ford's 429 Cobra Jet stood tall as well, as did cars like Plymouth's Superbird, AMC's Rebel Machine, and Oldsmobile's W-30 4-4-2. You almost couldn't swing a dead cat by the tail and not hit a red-hot musclecar.

Then along came the end of the road. Signs abounded even as the LS-6 was kicking ass and taking names in 1970. Safety crusaders and clean-air cops in Washington had been busy, too, and their work spelled the end for factory performance as we knew it 30-odd years back. To help meet tightening emissions standards to come, all automakers began cutting engine compression in 1971, and by the end of the year all the great musclecar mills were history. Somehow Pontiac managed to keep building excitement, offering its amazing emissions-legal, yet-still-hot 455 Super Duty Firebird in 1973 and '74. But that was about it.

Apparently it was only right that the company that kicked off the fastest 10 years in Detroit history also close things down. For then. Fortunately American muscle is back and better than ever today.

Today's high-performance is stronger than ever

Who said there's no such thing as a time machine? When the great American musclecar faded away in the early Seventies, most gearheads were sure they'd never see such fast times again. And for nearly 15 years or so, it looked like they were right. But look around you now. The musclecar did make a comeback and today takes Americans on wild rides that, in some cases, are not only reminiscent of those heady days in the Sixties but actually go far beyond what was then considered strong.

Modern muscle of the new millennium is truly multi-faceted; cars like Z06 Corvettes, Dodge Vipers and supercharged Mustang Cobras can stop as well as they start and handle the curves with every bit as much machismo as they demonstrate on the straight and narrow. Along with that, they're also relatively practical—compared, say, to an old 427 Cobra or L88 Corvette—and they're not at all that bad on fuel. It's kinda like having your cake and eating, too—at 140 miles per hour or more.

How'd Detroit's automakers do it? By playing with the cards they were dealt. It was only a matter of time before designers and engineers, being relatively smart people, caught up with hurdles placed before them by the likes of environmental-minded legislatures and price-gouging fuel moguls. Easily the greatest technological advance along the way to the musclecar's rebirth was the development of electronic fuel delivery systems—computer controls to you. Carburetors may have been cool, but there was only one way to perfect performance in all facets simultaneously, and that was to let a lightning-quick computer make all the decisions.

Of course, other things—advanced metallurgy, superior tire technology, much more precise manufacturing practices, etc.—have also contributed to the return of true high-performance. But suffice it to say simply enough that driving today is much more fun that it was 20 years back. Pontiac these days is even building a new GTO—a car that just might take some drivers back again to 1964.

1955 *Chrysler* C-300

Don't laugh, but this big beautiful luxury cruiser just may have been America's first musclecar. Born almost 10 years before Pontiac introduced its GTO, the first of Chrysler's famed "letter-cars" appeared in January 1955 and instantly wowed the world with it fabulous combination of serious speed and posh prestige.

Styling chief Virgil Exner had already spent a hundred million bucks remaking the corporation's 1955 models when chief engineer Robert MacGregor Rodger came up with the letter-car idea. Exner liked Rodger's idea, as did Chrysler division manager Ed Quinn, who gave the go-ahead as long as costs were kept down. The buck was then passed on to Cliff Voss, head of the Chrysler Imperial design studio, who, along with Rodger and production chief Tom Piorier, managed to pull off the feat in classic fashion.

Combining some lavish Imperial features with the hot 331 cubic-inch "hemi" V8, Chrysler's first letter car was named for its output rating of 300 horsepower. Officially the car was labeled the "C-300," undoubtedly in honor of Briggs Cunningham's various hemi-powered LeMans racers of 1951-54, all of which were identified by an appropirate "C" prefix. When a second letter-series Chrysler showed up in 1956 it was tagged the "300B," and thus began a progression

that followed in alphabetical order for each year to follow. With the exception of omitting the letter "I," supposedly to avoid confusion with the Roman numeral "I," Chrysler's letter car legacy carried on through 11 model runs, ending in 1965 with the 300L.

Based on a New Yorker hardtop bodyshell, the 1955 C-300 mounted an attractive egg-crate Imperial grille and understated Windsor bodyside trim. Inside was a padded dashboard, a 150-mph speedometer, and tan leather appointments. Rodger's contribution was the 300-horse hemi with its twin Carter four-barrel carbs, high-lift cam, solid lifters, 8.5:1 compression and dual low-restriction exhausts.

Built as "a sports touring car designed to bring Chrysler the benefit of a high-performance reputation," the C-300 did not disappoint. Even as big and heavy as it was, it could still run almost as fast as Chevrolet's new V8 Corvette. According to Mechanix Illustrated scribe Tom McCahill, the '55 C-300 was "the most powerful sedan in the world, and the fastest, teamed up with rock-crushing suspension and a competition engine capable of yanking Bob Fulton's steamboat over the George Washington Bridge." With that established, McCahill continued on, explaining that "this is definitely not the car for Henrietta Blushbottom, your maiden schoolmarm aunt, to use for hustling up popsicles. This is a hard-boiled, magnificent piece of semi-competition transportation, built for the real automotive connoisseur."

Semi-competition? Chrysler's first 300 went right to the track with ease, first setting a flying-mile speed record of 127.58 mph on the beach at Daytona. Next came complete domination of NASCAR and AAA stock-car racing in 1955 thanks to the factory-sponsored efforts of Carl Kiekhaefer's Mercury Outboards racing team. On the NASCAR circuit, Tim Flock

Right: *Tim Flock's C-300 in action on Daytona's old beach/ road course. Flock and his Chrysler were runaway NASCAR champs in 1955.*

Opposite page: *Chrysler's C-300 established all-new precedents for performance and prestige.*

Below: *In 1954, the Firepower hemi V8 produced 235 horsepower, 55 ponies more than it had delivered when introduced in 1951.*

won 13 consecutive Grand National races at the wheel of his Kiekhaefer 300 on the way to copping the season title. Another Kiefhaefer Chrysler, driven by Frank Mundy, won the AAA crown. In all, Chrysler 300s won 37 stock car races in 1955. Another 22 NASCAR wins followed for the 300B in 1956 as Buck Baker's Kiekhaefer Chrysler took the championship. The dominating Kiefkhaefer team was then broken up in December 1956.

Chrysler's beautiful brute kept on rolling strong even after it retired from racing. After becoming America's first car to offer more than one horsepower per cubic inch (by way of the optional 355-horse 354 hemi) in 1956, the 300 remained among Detroit's most powerful offerings. Optional output in 1957 hit 390 horsepower; it reached the 400 mark in 1960. But with the Sixties came the modern musclecar wave, led by the GTO. The 300 letter cars became dinosaurs once speed-sensitive Americans began flocking to this new breed of mid-sized performance machines. Although sales were brisk for the 300K and 300L in 1964 and '65, the decision was still made to honorably end the legacy on a high note before the handwriting on the wall became any more obvious.

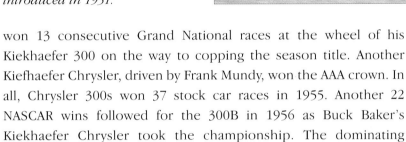

CHRYSLER V-8 FIREPOWER "235" ENGINE

MILESTONE FACTS

- The "C" in "C-300" probably was an honorary reference to legendary international racer Briggs Cunningham, who had used Chrysler hemi-head V8s in various competition cars during the early Fifties.

- The name "300" came from the car's unprecedented power output. Save for a few very rare, very expensive Duesenberg's built before World War II, the '55 C-300 was America's first car to come standard with 300 horsepower.

- Chrysler's letter-series models were built for 11 years. Following the C-300 of 1955 came the 300B in 1956, the 300C in 1957, the 300D in 1958, and so on up to the 300L in 1965.

- The letter "I" was skipped in 1964 to avoid confusion with the Roman numeral "I."

- All Chrysler 300 models built in 1955 were two-door coupes fitted with Powerflite automatic transmissions; a convertible version was introduced in 1957.

- Only three color choices were available for the C-300 in 1955: Tango Red, Chrysler Platinum White and black.

- Power brakes, leather upholstery, a custom steering wheel and full wheelcovers were standard. Dazzling wire wheels and power steering were optional, as was a power seat.

By then, Chrysler officials already knew that most American would soon be forgetting which car truly originated the musclecar craze. No, baby-boomers, it wasn't the GTO.

Chrysler 300 tailfins were modest in 1955. They would soar in 1957.

Unique door handles represented just one of many elegant touches on the car later called the "beautiful brute."

Chrysler's first "letter-car" took its name (left) from its output rating: 300 horsepower. A 150-mph speedometer (right) was standard.

SPECIFICATIONS

Wheelbase: 126 inches

Weight: 4,005 pounds

Base price: $4,360

Engine: 300-horsepower 331-cid Firepower "Hemi" OHV V8

Induction: two Carter four-barrel carburetors

Transmission: two-speed Powerflite automatic

Suspension: independent A-arms w/coil springs in front, live axle with leaf springs in back

Brakes: four-wheel hydraulic drums

Performance: 0-60 in 9.5 seconds, quarter-mile in 17.6 seconds at 82 mph

Production: 1,725, including exports.

Flashy deluxe wheelcovers were standard on the C-300. Dazzling wire wheels were optional.

1961 *Chevrolet* SS 409

Chevrolet was the first to offer real horsepower to the masses in 1955. Then the guys who brought you "The Hot One" followed that up six years later with its fabled "409," the potent powerplant that overnight had everyone singing its praises. Most notable were the lyrics released by "The Beach Boys" in May 1962.

"She's real fine, my four-or-nine," began Brian Wilson's epic tune, which would be remembered long after the engine itself faded away into the automotive archives.

The 409 tale dates back to 1958 when Chevrolet introduced its 348-cubic-inch V8, often called a "W-head" because of the pattern made by its alternating valve positions. Look down on top of a 348 cylinder head and the valves traced out a "W"—or an "M" depending on your relative position. Many today still think the 409 was simply a bored-and-stroked 348, but the leap from one to the other wasn't anywhere near that easy.

First and foremost, boring out the 348 block was not suggested—there wasn't enough cast-iron in place between the water jacket and cylinders. Engineers had to recast the block to increase the bore, then they stretched the stroke to produce the displacement that fit so well in Wilson's song.

From there, modifications were plenty, so much so that swapping parts between the 348 and 409 was basically out of the question. New forged aluminum pistons featured centered wrist pins and symmetrical valve reliefs milled straight across the piston top in pairs. Their 348 counterparts had offset wrist pins and one large intake relief, one smaller exhaust relief, meaning two opposite sets of four pistons were required. All 409 pistons interchanged regardless of which cylinder bank they belonged to.

Improved components for the 409 included a beefed-up forged steel crank; shortened, reinforced connecting rods; and more durable aluminum bearings. Heads were also specially cast to accept larger diameter pushrods and machined on top for heavier valve springs. The 409's solid-lifter cam was also much more aggressive than its 348 cousin.

Happily feeding hefty gulps of fuel/air mixture was a large Carter AFB four-barrel carburetor on an aluminum intake, equipment that flowed every bit as strongly as the triple-carb setup used by the top-shelf 348s. A Delco-Remy ignition featuring a dual-breaker, centrifugal-advance distributor sparked that mixture, and spent gases were hauled away by low-restriction iron manifolds. Output was 360 horsepower.

IT FEELS GOOD, LOOKS BETTER and GOES GREAT!

Take any one of Chevy's five '61 Impalas, add either the new 409-cubic-inch V8 or the 348-cubic-inch job and a four-speed floor-mounted stick, wrap the whole thing in special trim that sets it apart from any other car on the street, and man, you have an Impala Super Sport! Every detail of this new Chevrolet package is custom made for young men on the move. This is the kind of car the insiders mean when they say <u>Chevy</u>, the kind that can only be appreciated by a man who understands, wants, and won't settle for less than REAL driving excitement.

Here are the ingredients of the Impala Super Sport kit* • Special Super Sport trim, inside and out • Instrument Panel Pad • Special wheel covers • Power brakes and power steering • Choice of five power teams: 305 hp. with 4-speed Synchro-Mesh or heavy-duty Powerglide. 340 hp. with 4-speed only. 350 hp. with 4-speed only. 360 hp. with 4-speed only • Heavy-duty springs and shocks • Sintered metallic brake linings • 7,000-RPM Tach • 8.00 x 14 narrow band whitewalls • Chevrolet Division of General Motors, Detroit 2, Michigan.

*Optional at extra cost, as a complete kit only.

MAY, 1961

A mandatory supporting cast for the 409 included a 3.36:1 rear axle and a four-speed manual transmission. Powerglide and air conditioning reportedly were not available, but power steering and brakes were, as was an all-important positraction differential. Over-the-counter optional rear gears (running as low as 4.56:1) were also offered.

Right: *Wildly upholstered bucket seats showed up on a 1961 Impala showcar. All 1961 Super Sports came with a front bench.*

Opposite page: *Chevy's first SS model represented the best combination of performance and pizzazz ever seen by Average Joe Carbuyer.*

Most interesting on the options list was the Super Sport kit. Introduced shortly after the 409 appeared, the SS equipment was born basically to showcase the king of the W-heads. Included was an awfully nice collection of imagery and performance equipment.

On the outside, tri-blade spinner wheelcovers caught the eye, and the attraction was further enhanced inside with a padded dashboard and a Corvette-type grab bar atop the glove box opening. A 7000-rpm tachometer, mounted on the steering column, was standard, as was an exclusive dress-up floor plate for four-speed Super Sports. "SS" identification inside and out completed the show. But there was more.

Underneath, Limited Production Optiona (LPO) number 1108, the police handling package, added a stiffer sway bar up front, sintered-metallic brake linings, and heavy-duty springs and shocks all around. Power steering and brakes and 8.00x14 narrow-band whitewall tires were included, too.

Overall, the 409 SS Impala looked and played the part of a truly hot car as well as anything Detroit had to offer in 1961. Rest to 60 mph took only seven seconds or so, and the metallic brakes were an able match for that power. Meanwhile, the police chassis did a nice job of apprehending body roll and keeping the 3,700-pond Super Sport dirty-side down. Wrapping things up was an image that screamed "cool" every bit as loud as the exhaust notes backing up "The Beach Boys" on their big 1962 hit.

The 1961 Impala SS kicked off Chevrolet's legendary SS legacy, a bloodline that would eventually branch out to practically anything on four wheels wearing a Bow-Tie badge. And although the 409, like its 348 forefather, would soon itself become an antique, for a few short years it was the machine many performance buyers were saving their pennies and dimes for.

To some nostalgic baby-boomers, she's still real fine.

MILESTONE FACTS

- Chevrolet built the 409 up through 1965 before it was superseded by Chevrolet's all-new Mk IV big-block V8 displacing 396 cubic inches.

- Brochures claimed the Super Sport Kit could be ordered on any model in 1961, including four-doors. No such applications, however, are known.

- The Impala SS legacy ran strong until 1969. It was later reborn in 1994, this time based on the four-door Caprice platform.

- The 409 V8 was a derivation of the 348, which explains why more than one wag over the years has labeled the former a "truck engine." The latter, when introduced in 1958, was indeed targeted for Chevrolet's truck line, though it also appeared as the top-performance engine option for the passenger-car line until 1961.

- A 409-horsepower 409 V8 option was introduced very late in the 1961 model run.

- Only Chevy's baddest big-blocks, the 348 and 409, were offered for the Impala SS in 1961. In 1962, Super Sport buyers could also pick the 235-cid six-cylinder and 283 and 327 small-blocks.

- Output for the 409 V8 topped out at 425 horsepower in 1963.

- From 1961 to '63, the Impala SS was an options package. Then the full-sized Super Sport gained individual model-line status in 1964. Total production that year soared to 185,325.

Chevy's sport coupe body with its large rear window (above) was the perfect base for the 1961 Super Sport. Special SS badging appeared on the deck lid (left), and spinner hubcaps (upper right) were also standard.

SPECIFICATIONS

Wheelbase: 119 inches

Weight: 3,737 pounds

Original price: $3,500, approximately

Engine: 409 cubic-inch "W-head" V8

Induction: single Carter four-barrel carburetor

Compression: 11.25:1

Horsepower: 360 at 5,800 rpm

Torque: 409 at 3,600 rpm

Transmission: Muncie four-speed manual

Suspension: independent A-arms w/coil springs in front; four-link live axle with coil springs in back

Brakes: four-wheel drums

Performance: 14.2 seconds at 98.14 mph in the quarter-mile, according to Motor Trend

Production: 453 Impala Super Sports with both engines, 348 and 409—409 V8 production is listed at 142 with no breakdown given as to model (some went into Bel Airs, Biscaynes, etc.)

Four-speed Super Sports were treated to a bright floor-shifter surround (upper left). A 7000-rpm column-mounted tachometer (above) was standard on all SS models, whether automatic or manual-equipped.

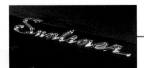

1961 *Ford Sunliner* 390-6V V8

It was a battle for the ages, Ford vs. Chevy; the former poised to finally catch the latter in Detroit's sales race after following for far too long. The year was 1957, and horsepower was a prime selling point. Chevrolet's "Hot One," the high-winding, overhead-valve small-block V8 introduced to raves in 1955, was getting hotter by the year.

New for '57 was optional fuel-injection, which could boost output for the newly enlarged 283-cube small-block all the way up to 283 horses. Ford engineers, meanwhile, were bolting dual-carb setups and even Paxton superchargers onto their 312 cubic-inch Y-block V8. Both companies had NASCAR tracks in mind when they developed these parts as Detroit's automakers were now well aware of the promotional value of a race-winning reputation.

But hold your horses... In June the Automobile Manufacturers Association enacted its "ban" on factory racing involvement, supposedly to help demonstrate Detroit's new awareness of automotive safety issues. Actually, the AMA edict was probably more of a ploy used by its chairman, Red Curtice, to undercut Ford's efforts to one-up Chevrolet. Curtice was also president of General Motors. A mere coincidence? We think not. Whatever the case, Ford followed the AMA ban to the letter, while cheaters like Chevrolet and Pontiac continued promoting (albeit somewhat clandestinely) their performance programs like nothing had changed.

Dearborn-bred performance then suffered for two years before the Blue-Oval boys finally decided to get back in the race late in 1959. First came the 360-horse 352-cid Interceptor Special FE-series V8—Ford's first modern musclebound mill—as an option for 1960 models. That was followed up by an even larger FE, the 390, in 1961. Fed by single a four-barrel carburetor, the top-dog 390 that year was rated at 375 horsepower. All that oomph translated into 158.8 mph on Ford's test track in Romeo, Michigan, and a flying-mile speed record of 159.320 mph at Daytona Beach down Florida way.

But that wasn't all... "In 1960, Ford answered the complaints of dyed-in-the-wool enthusiasts who were tired of watching the competition disappear in the distance by introducing a 352-inch, 360-horsed high-performance V8," wrote Hot Rod's Ray Brock. "For 1961, they stepped up the tempo with a 390-inch V8 rated at 375 horsepower. Now here a few months later is another shot in the arm for Ford owners."

That poke in the shoulder was Ford's "6V induction system," the "6V" referring to the six throats of this new option's three Holley two-barrel carburetors, which dropped right down in place of the 375-horse 390's single-carb intake. Available only as a dealer-installed option, the 6V setup was reportedly delivered to your friendly neighborhood Ford store boxed up in the trunk of said 375-horse car. The switch was then made right before a buyer's eyes and bingo, an instant boost to 401 horsepower. Price for the 6V option was $260.

Among the first to take advantage of this deal was drag racer Les Ritchey. He took the three Holleys out of his '61 Ford's trunk and went racing at the 1961 NHRA Winternationals, managing a best run of 13.33 seconds at 105.50 mph at the wheel of his 401-horse Ford. Mean indeed for a two-ton brute.

MILESTONE FACTS

- When the AMA "anti-racing" edict was enacted in the summer of 1957, Ford overnight cancelled its high-performance options, including its supercharged 312 V8.

- In April 1959, Ford finally announced it would be offering high-performance options again with hopes of making up lost ground to Chevrolet and Pontiac.

- Engineers in 1961 bored and stroked the existing 352 cubic-inch FE-series big-block, resulting in the 390 V8.

- Ford used the "4V" label to describe their four-barrel V8s, the "V" being short for venturi. The company's triple two-barrel induction setup then logically became the "6V."

- The 390-6V V8 was Ford's first engine to surpass 400 advertised horsepower.

- Lee Iacocca took over as Ford general manager in November 1960.

- Advertisements called the 1961 Fords "The Lively Ones."

- Ford named its 401-horsepower triple-carb V8 the "Thunderbird Special." Its official engine code was "Z."

Ford's hottest 390 V8s were offered beneath the hoods of all 1961 models save station wagons—thus the 401-horse Sunliner convertible shown here. Introduced midyear in 1961 as well was Ford's first modern four-on-the-floor, a Borg-Warner T-10 four-speed manual transmission. This Sunliner, however, features the more typical T-85 three-speed, which was "standard" behind the 375- and 401-horse 390 V8s. Like the triple-carb option, the T-10 four-speed was a dealer-installed option only.

Typical foundation fortification came along with any 1961 Ford fitted with either the 375- or 401-horse 390 (both engines used the same ordering code, "Z"), beginning with typically beefed springs and shock absorbers. Also included were bigger brakes with three-inch wide shoes, an oversized three-inch diameter driveshaft incorporating tougher U-joints, high-speed Firestone nylon tires on 15-inch wheels, and a four-pinion differential.

In 1962, both the triple-carb intake and four-speed stick went from dealer-installed items to true factory-delivered options. New that year too was an even larger FE, the 406, which then morphed the following year into the famed 427... That, however, is another story.

Left: *The skinny treads used in the early Sixties didn't stand a chance against Ford's 401-horse triple-carb V8.*

A column-shifted three-speed manual gearbox was standard behind the 390-6V big-block V8 in 1961.

Sunliner convertibles in 1961 were treated to Ford's top-shelf Galaxie-line trim treatment, which included stone shields behind each rear wheel.

Adding three Holley two-barrel carbs to Ford's 390-cid FE-series V8 in 1961 upped the output ante from 375 horses to 401.

SPECIFICATIONS

Wheelbase: 209.9 inches

Weight: 3,694 pounds

Base Price (for V8 Sunliner convertible): $2,847

Engine: 390 cubic-inch FE-series V8

Compression: 10.6:1

Induction: three Holley two-barrel carburetors on an aluminum intake manifold

Horsepower: 401 at 6,000 rpm

Torque: 430 at 3,500 rpm

Transmission: column-shifted Borg-Warner T-85 three-speed manual

Suspension: independent A-arms w/coil springs in front; live axle with leaf springs in back; springs, brakes and shocks were all special heavy-duty pieces

Brakes: heavy-duty four-wheel drums

The Starliner coupe and Sunliner convertible were the flagships of the Galaxie series in 1961. Each received appropriate fender badges.

1962 *Pontiac* 421 Super Duty

No one, off the beach or otherwise, ever sang a note about this car, perhaps because saving pennies and dimes in this case would've got you nowhere fast. The engine along cost around $1,300, a bunch of bucks today, a small fortune 40 years back. But its sky-high price notwithstanding, nothing beat a Super Duty Pontiac in 1962. Nothing, not even a 409.

Designed to do battle on dragstrips and stock-car tracks, Pontiac's 421 Super Duty Catalina was never meant for polite society, which makes comparison between toned-down super-stock rivals from Ford and Chevrolet akin to squaring off apples and oranges. Like those Max Wedge Mopars also introduced in 1962, the 421 SD Catalina was an all-out factory super stock, plain and simple. Base 406 Fords and 409 Chevys in 1962 could've been driven on the street with relative ease; anyone who tried to tame a 421 Super Duty that year was in for a tough time. "These cars are not intended for general passenger car use," read a corporate disclaimer, "and they are not supplied by Pontiac Motor Division for such purposes."

Super Duty roots run back to December 1959 with the introduction of various high-performance parts intended to put Pontiac out in front on NASCAR tracks. Rated at 363 horsepower, the 389 cubic-inch Super Duty V8 proved its worth at Daytona in February 1960 when Fireball Roberts' Pontiac lapped the superspeedway at a then-incredible 155 mph. Output for the 389 SD was upped to 368 horses in 1961, helping Pontiac pull off a 1-2-3 finish at Daytona. In all, Super Duty Pontiacs copped 30 of 52 NASCAR races that year.

After a bore job in late 1961, the 421-cube Super Duty picked right up where the 389 variety left off. Motor Trend's Roger

Huntington went for a ride in one with Pontiac ad-man Jim Wangers in January 1962, and he couldn't say enough about the car's outrageous performance: "Wangers got into that big Poncho, and we went. Low gear was a rubber-burning fishtail. A snap shift to 2nd at 5500 rpm and 60 mph came up in a bit over five seconds. Second and 3rd gears almost tore my head off. Then across the finish line in high at 5300—stopping the watch at 13.9 ad 107 mph. Acceleration figures like these are not uncommon in Super/Stock classes on our dragstrips. But when you can turn them with a car just the way you buy it, you have something to scream about."

Purpose built from air cleaner to oil pan as a certified super-stock screamer, the 421 Super Duty featured a beefy four-bolt block with a forged steel crank and 11:1 compression Mickey Thompson forged aluminum pistons. An aggressive #10 "McKellar" cam (named after Pontiac's fast-thinking engineer Malcolm McKellar) activated big valves (1.92-inch intake, 1.76 exhaust) through solid lifters and 1.65:1 rockers. Two big Carter AFB carbs, with a total flow of 1000 cfm, sat atop an aluminum intake. And spent gases were hauled away by a pair of intriguing cast-iron, individual-runner "long branch" headers incorporating convenient cutouts for wide-open running.

Additional track-ready Super Duty fare included various lightweight body parts. Steel could've been traded for weight-saving aluminum for the hood, front bumper, fenders, inner fenders and radiator brackets. Pontiac was the first to offer weight-saving components for its factory super-stocks, but by the end of 1962 all of Detroit was in the aluminum (or fiberglass) game.

Exotic optional aluminum exhaust manifolds helped trim the fat, too, as did a special frame that featured perimeter rails that were cut out to transform rectangular tubes into channel. A customer also could have specified the deletion of insulation and sound deadener, but only a handful did.

MILESTONE FACTS

- Pontiac built 200 405-horse 421 Super Duty V8s in 1962 to satisfy new NHRA drag racing rules specifying that a factory could only legalize a particular engine for its dragstrips by selling it in "regular-production" form to the public. Of these SD engines, at least 179 made into 1962 Pontiac models.

- Among the 421 Super Duty V8's race-ready standard features were deep-grooved pulleys and a high-volume oil pump. A deep-sump eight-quart oil pan was optional.

- A column-shifted Borg-Warner T-85 three-speed manual was standard behind the 421 Super Duty V8. A T-10 four-speed was optional

- Surprisingly, 16 421 Super Duty V8s were installed in luxury-minded Grand Prix coupes in 1962.

- Super Duty Pontiacs were built again early in 1963 before General Motors executives ordered all of its divisions to cease their involvement in racing projects.

- Super Duty exhaust manifolds, known as "long branch" headers, featured individual runners that led to two openings, one the flowed into an exhaust pipe, another that could be opened up for non-restrictive operation. These cast-iron manifolds were also available in lightweight aluminum form.

- Heavy-duty 11-inch finned aluminum front brake drums were optional for the Super Duty Catalina, as were 4.30:1 rear gears.

- Catalinas typically rolled on 14-inch wheels in 1962. Adding the heavy-duty brake package to a Super Duty model brought along bigger 15-inch wheels.

Other options included a Safe-T-Track differential with a wide range of gear ratios, bullet-proof axles, beefier brakes with larger 15-inch wheels, stiffer springs and shocks, front and rear sway bars, and all of Pontiac's popular style and appearance packages, such as the attractive eight-lug rims and sporty Venture trim group with its tri-tone "Morrokide" upholstery. Though dressing up a Super Duty wasn't the idea, at least 16 customers in 1962 thought it might be cool to combine the savage Super Duty V8 with the sensual Grand Prix coupe, in its first year as one of Detroit's sexiest luxo-cruisers.

Nearly all other Super Duty cars, however, went right to the track, where they dominated NASCAR racing yet again in 1962. And those that did find their way onto the street had many a foolish stoplight challenger singing the blues. As Roger Huntington explained further after his wild ride, "I must say, [the] 421 Pontiac is a terrific piece of automobile. I'm still shaking."

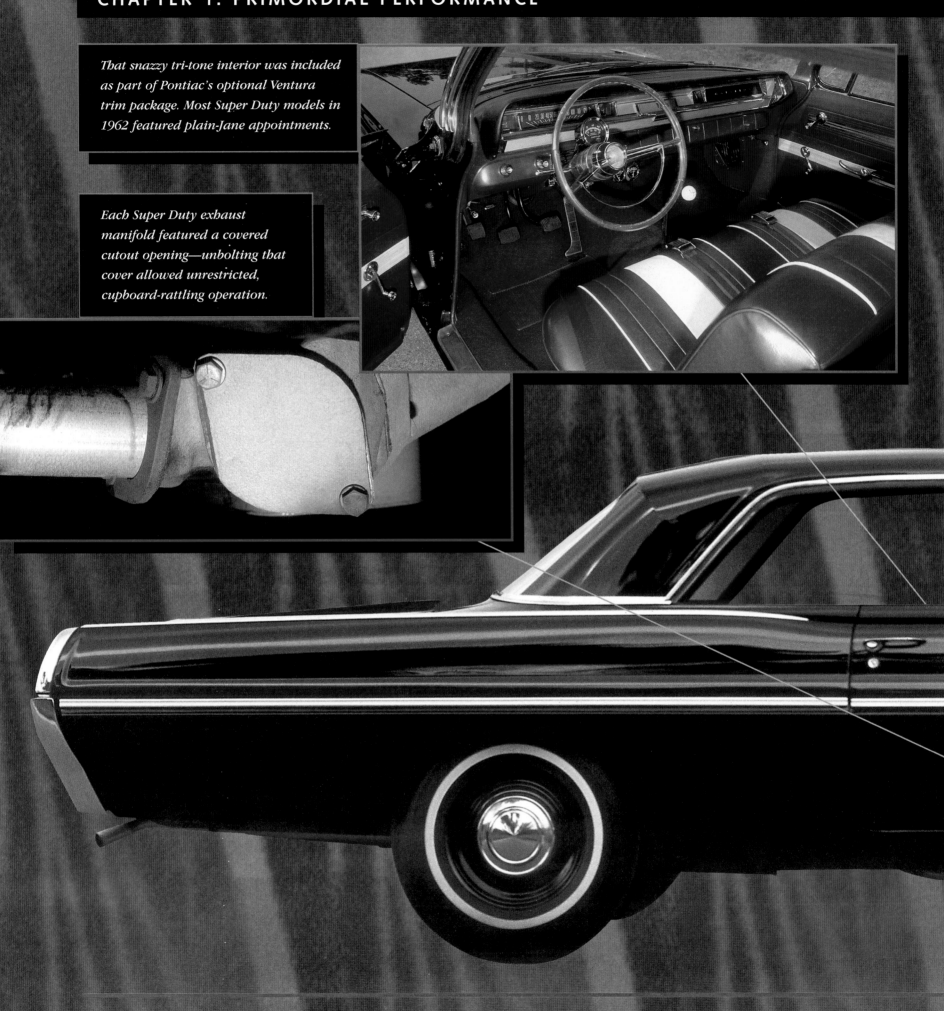

That snazzy tri-tone interior was included as part of Pontiac's optional Ventura trim package. Most Super Duty models in 1962 featured plain-Jane appointments.

Each Super Duty exhaust manifold featured a covered cutout opening—unbolting that cover allowed unrestricted, cupboard-rattling operation.

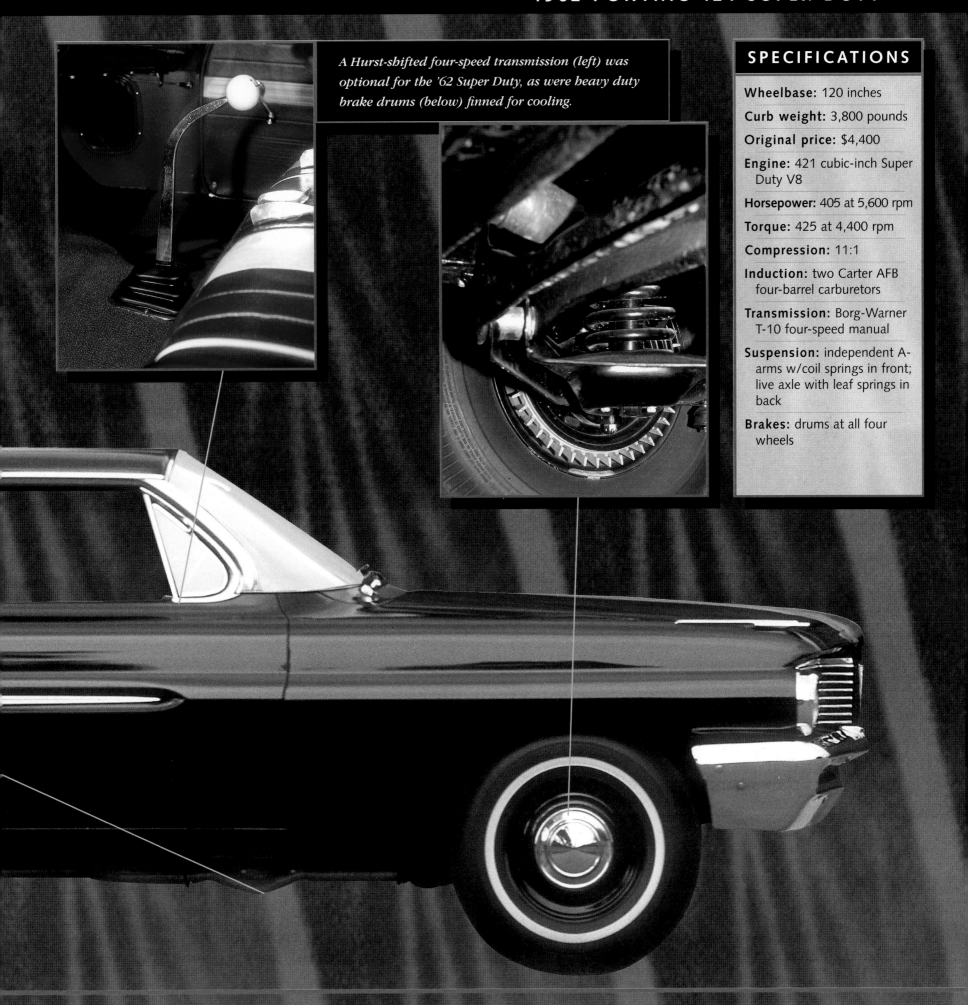

A Hurst-shifted four-speed transmission (left) was optional for the '62 Super Duty, as were heavy duty brake drums (below) finned for cooling.

SPECIFICATIONS

Wheelbase: 120 inches

Curb weight: 3,800 pounds

Original price: $4,400

Engine: 421 cubic-inch Super Duty V8

Horsepower: 405 at 5,600 rpm

Torque: 425 at 4,400 rpm

Compression: 11:1

Induction: two Carter AFB four-barrel carburetors

Transmission: Borg-Warner T-10 four-speed manual

Suspension: independent A-arms w/coil springs in front; live axle with leaf springs in back

Brakes: drums at all four wheels

1962 *Dodge Polara* 413 *Max Wedge*

Chevy's 409 wasn't the only Detroit hot rod immortalized in song by the Beach Boys. In March 1963 Brian Wilson and crew cut "Shut Down," an automotive rhapsody in blue (smoke, that is) that told the tale of a street race between a fuel-injected Sting Ray and a 413 super-stock Dodge. The Corvette won, naturally.

Polara, intermediates of sorts riding on a shortened 116-inch wheelbase, down two inches from their 1961 forerunners. The downsized '62 Dart weighed roughly 3,400 pounds, a few hundred less than the full-sized Bel Airs, Catalinas and Galaxies. No weight-saving body parts made of aluminum or fiberglass were needed to take the new Dodge to the dragstrip.

Left: *Race-ready Max Wedge Mopars could break into the quarter-mile's 12-second bracket with ease.*

Below: *Wild free-flowing exhaust manifolds with special cutouts were Max Wedge features in 1962 and '63. Ghosted here is Dodge's 1963 rendition.*

B ut the race had to have been rigged; hands down, a "fuelie" Vette was no match for a "Max Wedge" Mopar.

That Max Wedge label was actually street slang for what Dodge officially called its "Ramcharger 413" V8—Plymouth's identical counterpart was the "Super Stock 413." "Max" came from the "Maximum Performance" designation used in factory brochures, while "Wedge" referred to the engine's wedge-shaped combustion chambers, as opposed to the hemi-heads already made famous by Chrysler. Introduced in May 1962 in response to Chevy's 409-horse 409 and Pontiac's big, bad 421 Super Duty, the Max Wedge 413 was built with one use in mind, and grocery-getting wasn't it.

The factory super-stock race was up and running full force by then and Chrysler Corporation was the last of the Big Three players to get off the line. But Mopar men wasted little time catching back up. Newly appointed corporate head Lynn Townsend had put part-time racer, full-time engineer Tom Hoover in charge of Chrysler's competition performance program in October 1961, and Hoover wasn't one to sit still long.

He and his engineers had one major building block in their favor. In Dodge terms, 1962 was the first year for the revamped Dart and

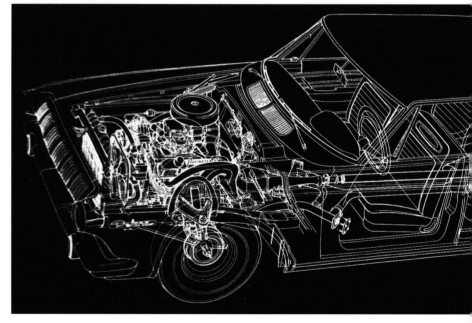

As for motivation, Hoover's team left no bolt unturned while overhauling the existing 413 V8 into a fire-breathing monster. About the only carryover was the block, and it was reportedly

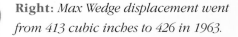

inspected for main-bearing ruggedness. Cylinder bores were also notched at the top to provide clearance for the 1.88-inch exhaust valves, which were more than a quarter-inch larger than standard issue. On the bottom end, a forged steel crankshaft with hardened journals and high-load tri-metal bearings did its part to support factory claims of 6,500-rpm potential. Magnafluxed forged steel rods and lightweight forged aluminum pistons assisted as well.

Back up top, the heads were redesigned to improve flow characteristics by 25 percent. They were also beefed up to help prevent gasket failure under high-compression conditions, and the heat crossover passage was eliminated to increase volumetric efficiency (a cooler intake charge is a denser intake charge). Additional valvetrain features included high-pressure dual valves springs with spiral steel dampers sandwiched between them to prevent harmful harmonics at high rpm. Though crucial to maximizing performance, the dual springs made it impossible to install oils seals on the valve stems, making the Max Wedge a serious oil-burner (wide-clearance piston rings also contributed).

A Max Wedge 413, of course, could also suck down the high-test, and that was supplied by a unique cross-ram aluminum intake sporting twin Carter AFB four-barrel car-buretors set on a diagonal. At the exhaust end were equally intriguing cast-iron manifolds that swept up and over the heads and dumped into a collector featuring cutouts with bolt-on covers. These covers easily slipped off for wide-open operation at the strip.

On the street a Max Wedge was a true killer. Roger Huntington's August 1962 Motor Trend road test produced a best run of 13.44 seconds at 109.76 mph for a slightly tweaked model. Obviously the

Right: Max Wedge displacement went from 413 cubic inches to 426 in 1963.

use of slicks and various other tricks allowed by stock-class racing rules promised even better times. Mid-12s were no problem on the strip, and a Max Wedge was eventually the first "production stock passenger car with a factory option engine" to break through the 12-second barrier.

Though initial plans called for building 200 Max Wedge cars (both Dodge and Plymouth) in 1962, demand reportedly upped the actual output figure by another 100 or so. Manufactured under precise conditions by Chrysler's Marine and Industrial Division, the Ramcharger 413 V8s were available in every 1962 Dodge model except station wagons. While most Max Wedge motors went into low-priced, stripped-down Dart sedans, at least a few were ordered beneath upscale Polara hoods, like the oddball shown on these pages.

A truly strange combination of poshness and performance, this beautiful brute clearly put the Max in Max Wedge.

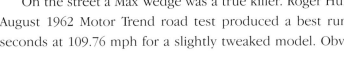

MILESTONE FACTS

- The term "Max Wedge" was street slang that applied to both Dodge and Plymouth models fitted with Chrysler Corporation's hot 413 super-stock V8.

- Dodge's Ramcharger 413 was available in two forms in 1962, one rated at 410 horsepower, the other at 420. Compression was 11:1 for the former, a molecule-mashing 13.5:1 for the latter.

- Motor Trend magazine's Roger Huntington called the Max Wedge's exhaust manifolds "a work of art—far and away the most efficient [system] ever put on an American car."

- Behind the Max Wedge 413 V8 in 1962 was either a heavy-duty Borg-Warner T-85 three-speed manual with a 10.5-inch clutch or the impressive A-727 Torqueflite three-speed automatic.

- Thanks to the durable Torqueflite, Max Wedge Dodges quickly became the runaway favorite in drag racings's Super Stock/Automatic classes.

- Additional Max Wedge Dodge features in 1962 included a heavy-duty driveshaft; beefy brakes, shocks and six-leaf rear springs, all taken from the police car parts shelf.

- Dodge's 420-horse 413 V8 came with specific instructions in 1962: "A final word of warning, the 13.5:1 engine must never be run at top speeds for more than 15 seconds at a time."

A Borg-Warner three-speed manual (right) or a Torqueflite automatic handled the horses handed off by a 1962 Max Wedge V8. Full-dress Polara trim (below) and snazzy interior appointments (far right) were not common to Dodge's Max Wedge. Most were bare-bones sedans.

Above: "Max Wedge" was actually street slang for Dodge and Plymouth's special 413 V8. In Dodge terms, the official name was "Ramcharger 413."

SPECIFICATIONS

Wheelbase: 116 inches

Weight: 3,500 pounds

Engine: 413 cubic-inch "Ramcharger 413" V8

Horsepower: 410 with 11:1 compression; 420 with 13.5:1

Induction: two Carter AFB (aluminum four-barrel) carburetors on an aluminum cross-ram manifold

Transmission: Borg-Warner T-85 three-speed manual

Suspension: independent A-arms w/coil springs in front; live axle with leaf springs in back

Brakes: four-wheel drums

Performance: 13.44 seconds at 109.76 mph for the quarter-mile (Motor Trend, August 1962)

Production: 300, estimated for both Dodge and Plymouth models

1964 *Pontiac* GTO

America's first modern musclecar, Pontiac's GTO, didn't become the performance segment's solid sales leader by being the fastest car on the road. The "Goat" emerged as an overnight marvel in 1964 because it represented an unprecedented combination of high performance and low cost that left even General Motors' conservative upper crust wondering where the hell all this fast-thinking was heading, as well as where it had come from.

Pontiac general manager Pete Estes had managed to sneak the supposedly taboo GTO past unwary corporate killjoys before they had a chance to do that voodoo that they did so well. Complaining company execs then shut up in a hurry after this hard charger hit the ground running in October 1963 and proceeded to take Detroit by storm.

The whole idea was so simple: take a lightweight car, drop in a big-block engine, bolt on a bit of heavy-duty hardware, and wrap it all up with a price tag readily within the reach of the baby boomer youth market then coming of age—presto, instant winner. Not only was that youth market just growing ripe for the picking at the time, but GM then was also preparing to unveil the right car for the job, the A-body intermediate.

A-bodies picked up where GM's so-called "senior compacts" left off, retaining the latter's existing nameplates while they were at it. Buick's Special, Oldsmobile's F-85 and Pontiac's Tempest were boosted up a notch into the new mid-sized ranks, where they were joined by Chevrolet's all-new Chevelle. Much bigger than a compact yet still smaller than the full-sized liners, these mid-sized models were relatively roomy yet comparatively light and agile. Most importantly, they could handle some serious V8 power, something their forerunners couldn't.

John DeLorean and fellow engineer Bill Collins at Pontiac had experimented with a big-block V8 Tempest in 1963, but the unit-body/rear-transaxle layout wasn't exactly designed with high performance in mind. That all changed, however, once the redesigned '64 Tempest came along with its full-perimeter frame and conventional solid rear axle.

Never one to overlook a chance to speed things up, Pontiac's ever-present advertising wizard, Jim Wangers, was already at work with DeLorean on a trend-setting performance package before the ink even dried on the A-body's blueprints. DeLorean had the engineering groundwork laid, while Wangers had his finger on the pulse of an excitable market poised to pounce on his powerful proposition. All

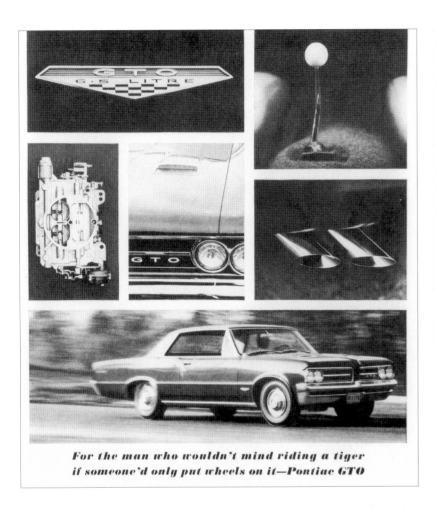

For the man who wouldn't mind riding a tiger if someone'd only put wheels on it—Pontiac GTO

MILESTONE FACTS

- The original GTO package initially was offered for the LeMans sports coupe and convertible. A hardtop then joined the mix soon after introduction.

- According to Car and Driver's David E. Davis in 1964, the new GTO "does what so many others only talk about—it really does combine brute, blasting performance with balance and stability of a superior nature."

- In 1964 and '65, the GTO came by way of an options group. In 1966 it was became transformed into its own individual model line.

- Car and Driver shocked its readers in 1964 with a road test that claimed the new GTO could run from rest to 100 mph in only 11.8 seconds. What the report didn't necessarily detail was their test car's many modifications, made by the guys at Royal Pontiac in Royal Oak, Michigan.

- The GTO's nicknames included "Goat," "The Tiger," and "The Great One."

- Total GTO production in 1964 was 32,450, including 6,644 convertibles

- GTO sales in 1975 soared beyond 75,000.

- Pontiac set the single-season musclecar sales high with 96,946 GTOs unleashed in 1966.

Above and left: *Pontiac's GTO hit the ground running in 1964 and remained Detroit's best-selling musclecar up through 1968.*

that remained was to sell the idea of a big-block intermediate to GM's top brass, a task that wouldn't be easy considering the corporation's anti-performance stance, as well as its 330 cubic-inch maximum displacement limit for its new mid-sized models.

Well aware of these roadblocks, Wangers and DeLorean made an end run. New models required corporate approval, but option packages didn't. They decided to quietly create a 389 option for the Tempest and worry about the consequences later. Of course, the plan would've never worked without Estes' support. But he loved the idea and went nose-to-nose with GM's disagreeable ivory tower execs to insure its success.

Credit for the name went to DeLorean, who unabashedly "borrowed" GTO from Enzo Ferrari. While purists cringed, the American public ate it up. Pontiac sales manager Frank Bridge predicted 1964 sales, at best, would reach 5,000. By the time the tire smoke cleared, 32,450 Goats had rolled out the door. Even

more could've been sold had the production line been able to keep up with demand.

Officially released on October 1, 1963, Pontiac's GTO debuted as an option package for the deluxe Tempest model, the LeMans. Coded W62, the option group included a 325-horse 389 V8 wearing pair of high-compression heads borrowed from the 389's big brother, the 421. Stiffer suspension and a three-speed manual were also part of the deal. Popular options included a Muncie four-speed and an even hotter 348-horse 389 topped by three Rochester two-barrel carbs, Pontiac's famed "Tri-Power" setup.

Pontiac's first GTO surely would have stood as the star of Detroit's 1964 show had not Ford chosen the same year to introduce its Mustang, a mass-market marvel if there ever was one. Nonetheless, Estes and crew weren't disappointed in the least; they had made their mark with the GTO, the car that first broke the rules then made new ones for the rest of Detroit to follow. That reality alone should be enough to allow Pontiac to take credit for the musclecar's conception.

Anyone out there want to argue?

SPECIFICATIONS

Wheelbase: 115 inches

Weight: 3,360 pounds

Original price: $3,400

Engine: 389 cubic-inch Tri-Power V8

Induction: three Rochester two-barrel carburetors

Compression: 10.75:1

Horsepower: 348 at 4,900 rpm

Torque: 428 at 3,600 rpm

Transmission: Hurst-shifted four-speed manual

Suspension: independent A-arms w/coil springs in front; live axle with coil springs in back

Brakes: drums front and rear

Performance: 14.30 seconds on the quarter-mile, according to Popular Hot Rodding

Production (with Tri-Power 389): 8,245, all models

Left: Stainless-steel Custom wheelcovers were optional for Pontiac's first GTO, as were bright exhaust tips.

Polite dress-up features included "GTO" identification, a blacked-out grille and twin dummy hood scoops.

1964 PONTIAC GTO

Below: The GTO legacy survived until 1974 then was revived 30 years later.

Above: When topped with Pontiac's famed "Tri Power" triple-carburetor option, the GTO's 389 cubic-inch V8 produced 348 horsepower.

1966 *Olds* 4-4-2 W-30

Oldsmobile entered the supercar sweepstakes in April 1964 with a performance machine that bore a name not everyone understood, even after early advertisements explained it in full. No, the moniker didn't read "Four-Forty-Two."

The proper pronunciation was "Four-Four-Two," as in four-barrel carburetor, four-on-the-floor and dual exhausts. Who cared that three-speed manuals and automatic transmissions soon found their way into the equation? The nameplate remained the same for 15 years and no one ever complained.

On each side of the center carb was a small square plate held down by two bolts. These plates served as valves for an internal crossover passage that typically allowed engine heat to make its way from the cylinder heads into the intake to enhance warm-up. By unbolting these plates, twisting them 90 degrees, and bolting them back down, a baffle on the plates' underside closed off the crossover passages. This helped the air/fuel mixture inside to stay cooler longer, and a cooler mixture is a denser mixture. Denser mixture is a key to making more horsepower on top end.

W-30 equipment in 1966 also included ram-air ductwork that fed cooler, denser outside air into those three Rochesters via two large plastic scoops situated in the openings in the front bumper normally reserved for turn signals, which were relocated farther inboard. Additional modifications included a slight reshaping (a tapered lip inside was flattened out to enlarge the space) of those openings to make way for the black plastic scoops—which reminded many wags of the business end of a vacuum cleaner. The jokes continued coming with a W-30's hood open as the two long, five-inch diameter flexible ducts running from the scoops to the unique chrome air cleaner looked as if they easily could've come right off of the wife's dryer.

Olds engineers stirred up the alpha-numeric pot even further in 1966, introducing their W-30 option, a ready-to-roll package meant to make the 4-4-2 the car to beat in super-stock drag racing. To that end, the original "W-machine" was offered only with the 4-4-2's strongest engine in 1966, the 400 cubic-inch L69 big-block V8. Introduced in November 1965, the 360-horse L69 featured three Rochester two-barrel carburetors on an intake that incorporated a clever little trick drag racers would immediately appreciate.

Two holes, probably cut by hand in 1966, were required in the radiator core support to allow safe passage for those ducts alongside the L69 V8. And with those two flex hoses taking up so

MILESTONE FACTS

- After building only 54 W-30 cars in 1966, Olds followed that with another 502 in 1967.

- L69 V8 installations in 1966 were not limited to W-30 cars. Total triple-carb 4-4-2 production that year was 2,129.

- The first-edition W-30's triple Rochester carburetors were superseded by a single four-barrel in 1967, per a General Motors' upper-office edict banning multiple-carb setups on all its divisions' cars save for the Corvette.

- An optional automatic transmission became available for the W-30 Olds in 1967.

- Lightweight inner fender wells up front—made of distinctive red plastic—became a W-30 trademark in 1967.

- In 1967 Oldsmobile paperwork first officially identified the W-30 package, labeling it the "Outside Air Induction" option.

- The best sales year for the W-30 Olds was 1970 when 3,100 hit the streets.

Opposite page: *Two black air inlets in the bumper below the headlights gave away a W-30 Oldsmobile's identity in 1966.*

Above: *The W-30 package carried on in similar fashion up through 1969. In 1970 the ram-air ductwork was replaced by a twin-scooped hood.*

much space beneath the W-30's hood, the battery had to be relocated rearward to the truck—a fortunate turn considering that's just where drag racers put theirs for improved weight transfer to the back wheels during hard acceleration. Trunk-mounted batteries were commonplace among factory super-stockers of the early Sixties, and this re-stowage would remain part of the W-30 plan in 1967.

Additional W-30 special equipment in 1966 included a four-bladed fan without a clutch, a heavy-duty three-core radiator, and a close-ratio four-speed manual transmission. Undoubtedly the most important component was the W-30's unique camshaft, a hydraulic, high-lift, long-duration unit that worked in concert with high-

tension chrome vanadium steel valve springs and dampers—a smaller spring within each spring helped inhibit oscillations and thus reduced the threat of valve float at high rpm. Compared to the "standard" L69 came with its 0.431/0.433 (intake/exhaust) inches of lift and 286 degrees duration, the W-30 shaft bumped both valves up 0.474 inch and featured 308 degrees of duration on both intake and exhaust. Though both this lumpy, rough-idling cam and the cool-air equipment obviously enhanced power potential, no output rating change was listed for the W-30 Olds.

Only 54 W-30 Oldsmobiles were sold in 1966, an understandably low figure considering the cars weren't promoted in the least. Official listings of the W-30 option didn't start showing up in factory paperwork until 1967, when production predictably jumped to 502. External identification was first added in 1969, though those barely noticeable "W-30" decals still did little to announce the arrival of Oldsmobile's hottest musclecar. Metal fender badges then replaced those decals in 1970 and were joined by a bold hood sporting two large intake scoops at its leading edge. By then, if you didn't know what "W-30" meant, you had no business on the street.

Oldsmobile's last "serious" W-30 package was offered in 1972. Though W-30 identification briefly reappeared in 1974 and '75, the translation wasn't quite the same. And the W-30 Oldsmobiles marketed in 1979 and '80 retained only the name, not the impact.

The W-30's battery was relocated from the crowded engine compartment to the trunk.

Simulated hood louvers (above) were standard on the 1966 4-4-2. Turn signals were relocated (right) to make room for the W-30's air ducts

Oldsmobile's triple-carb L69 V8 (right) was standard in the 1966 W-30. The 4-4-2 badge (below right) first appeared midyear in 1964.

SPECIFICATIONS

Wheelbase: 115 inches

Weight: 3,620 pounds

Engine: 400 cubic-inch L69 V8

Horsepower: 360 at 5,000 rpm

Induction: three Rochester two-barrel carburetors

Transmission: close-ratio Muncie four-speed manual

Suspension: independent A-arms w/coil springs in front; four-link live axle with coil springs in back

Brakes: four-wheel drums

Performance: N/A

Production: 54

1967 *Mercury Cyclone* 427

GTO clones were seemingly everywhere not long after Pontiac introduced the musclecar to the world in 1964. Oldsmobile's 4-4-2 appeared late that year, followed by Buick's Gran Sport and Chevrolet's SS 396 Chevelle in 1965. GM clearly had a great recipe cooking, but what about Chrysler and Ford?

While the two other Big Three players had the hot engines capable of running with the General's latest prime movers, the duo fell a bit short in the application department. Early on neither fielded a mid-sized muscle machine that matched up with the Goat or any of its corporate cousins.

At least Mercury tried. In January 1964, Ford's upscale corporate running mate introduced its Cyclone, a jazzed-up Comet wearing faux chrome-wheel wheelcovers, complete with chromed lug nuts. Bucket seats and console, a sporty three-spoke steering wheel, and a tach were included in the deal, which concentrated

more on imagery than action. Standard power was the Super Cyclone 289 small-block, rated at 210 horsepower.

Mercury's Cyclone whipped its way back on the scene in 1965 with all the same standard goodies offered the year before, plus an exclusive grille treatment. The Super Cyclone 289 also returned, now rated at 225 horses. Those 15 extras ponies, however, by no means improved the Cyclone's position compared to GM's big-block intermediates. According to Motor Trend, the best this baby could do in the quarter-mile was 17.1 seconds at 82 mph. Maybe that new optional fiberglass hood with its two simulated scoops would've helped.... Not.

Okay, so maybe those early Comet-based Cyclones constituted more hot air than hot performance. But Mercury had to start somewhere, and storm clouds were building even as the '65 Cyclone was blowing smoke up the tailpipes of rival musclecars. Although an optional 390-cube FE-series big-block appeared in 1966, it was still no match for the likes of Chevy's 396 and Pontiac's 400. Then came the answer to a fast-thinking Mercury man's prayers.

In 1966 Ford designers had started stuffing their biggest, baddest FE, the 427, into the Comet's mid-sized cousin, the Fairlane. From there the logic was almost impossible to miss. If the 427 fit into the Fairlane, it also could nestle between Cyclone flanks. Too bad it took a year for Mercury's movers and shakers to figure this one out.

For 1967, Comet customers were treated to two new big-block options, the 410-horsepower 427 with its single four-barrel carburetor and its 425-horse big brother, topped by two four-barrels. No production totals are available for the '67 427 Comet, but apparently at least eight 410-hp mid-sized Mercs were built that year, including the Jamaican Yellow Cyclone shown here. Like the 427 Fairlane, the 427 Mercury was created with drag racers in mind, leaving witnesses wondering why, in this case, a buyer would have opted for the top-shelf Cyclone coupe when he could have dropped the race-ready FE big-block into a cheaper, lighter, less frivolous base Comet sedan? Your guess is as good as ours—perhaps he wanted to be cooler than the competition at the strip.

Ordering the 427 option for the Cyclone in 1967 brought along a whole host of heavy-duty hardware, beginning with a knee-taxing 11.5-inch clutch. Behind that was a "top-loader" four-speed manual

Left: Save for easy-to-miss fender badges, no major external clues were present as to the 1967 427 Cyclone's true identity.

transmission that sent torque to a nodular 9-inch rearend filled with 31-spline axles and 3.89:1 non-locking gears. Additional additions included a heavy-duty battery, a 42-amp alternator, an extra-capacity radiator, and a clutch-fan.

FoMoCo's famous 427 need no introduction. But for those then living in caves, this beastly big-block was the same "side-oiler" engine that had taken no prisoners on NASCAR tracks in 1963 then followed that up with a milestone win at Le Mans three years later. Beneath a 427 Cyclone's hood in 1967 was the same cross-bolted block with its forged-steel crank, forged-steel Le Mans rods (with capscrews instead of bolts), and forged-aluminum pistons. Big valves, a bodacious solid-lifter cam and transistorized ignition were

MILESTONE FACTS

- Mercury's mid-sized lineup for 1967 began with the bare-bones Comet 202, the progressed up the pricing ladder to the Capri, the Caliente, and the Cyclone, which among other things came standard with bucket seats.

- Ford's FE-series big-block family was born in 1958. In 1961, maximum FE displacement went from 352 cubic inches to 390, followed by 406 in '62, and 427 in '63.

- The 427 powered Ford's GT-40 racing machine to a 1-2-3 finish at Le Mans in 1966.

- Engine code for the single-carb 410-hp 427 was "R." It was "W" for the 425-hp dual-carb variety.

- The king of the FE-series big-blocks actually displaced more like 425 cubic inches, but engineers labeled it a "427," probably to make sure it could never be topped in size by a rival. In those days, 7 liters—or about 427 cubic inches—was the common maximum displacement in most racing classes, and the biggest FE was built for racing, period.

- Only one 427 V8 option (fitted with a hydraulic-lifter cam and single-carb) was offered by Ford and Mercury in 1968 before being canceled midway through the model run. This 390-hp FE big-block was replaced by the 428 Cobra Jet V8 in April that year.

in there as well. A Holley four-barrel carb (with vacuum secondaries) fed things on top, and free-flowing cast-iron headers handled spent gases on the other end.

All told, the sum of these parts represented one of the meanest machines seen on the streets in 1967—a howling Cyclone if there ever was one.

Heavy-duty steel wheels adorned with no-nonsense "dog-dish" hubcaps were included when the 427 big-block was ordered for a 1967 mid-sized Mercury

Above: A single four-barrel carburetor fed the 410-horsepower 427 in 1967.

Left: Fitting a 1967 Merc with a 427 was done solely with competition in mind, and neither a radio or heater were needed at a dragstrip.

Right: Ford Motor Company's famed 427 cubic-inch FE-series V8 was born in 1963. It last appeared in 1968.

SPECIFICATIONS

Wheelbase: 116 inches

Weight: 3,600 pounds

Original Price: $4,100

Engine: 427 cubic-inch FE-series V8

Induction: single Holley four-barrel carburetor

Compression: 11.1:1

Horsepower: 410 at 5,600 rpm

Torque: 476 at 3,400 rpm

Transmission: four-speed "top-loader" manual

Suspension: independent A-arms w/coil springs in front; live axle with leaf springs in back

Brakes: power front discs, rear drums

Production (with 410-hp 427 V8): 8

1967 *Chevy Corvette* L-88

Of the many mean and nasty Corvettes unleashed during the half-century history of "America's Sportscar," among the meanest was the fabled L-88, built in limited numbers from 1967 to '69. Only 20 rolled out of Chevrolet's St. Louis assembly plant that first year, all clearly targeted for the track.

Anyone who tried to drive an L-88 on the street—and some fools did—were in for a rude awakening. For starters, there was no radio, heater, automatic choke, or fan shroud to aid underhood cooling. Also missing on the L-88, as was any semblance of emissions controls. A typical PCV valve wasn't even present; instead the 427 cubic-inch L-88 V8 used an obsolete road-draft tube that vented crankcase vapors directly into the atmosphere. Anything that wasn't needed on a race track, anything that added unwanted extra pounds, wasn't included in the L-88 package, an off-road option if there ever was one.

What was included was an impressive list of purposeful hardware, beginning with the L-88 427's weight-saving aluminum cylinder heads. Feeding things on top was a huge 850-cfm Holley four-barrel carb mounted on an open-plenum aluminum intake manifold that totally sacrificed low-speed cooperation for high-rpm flying. Atop all that was a unique air cleaner assembly that mated up with the Corvette's first functional ram-air hood. Ductwork bonded to the hood's underside directed air flow from the high-pressure area normally created at the base of any car's windshield into the hungry Holley below.

Remaining standard L-88 features contributed further to the car's gnarly nature. All L-88 Corvettes built in 1967 were fitted with such mandatory options as the stiff F41 suspension, G81 Positraction differential, J56 power-assisted metallic brakes, and M22 "Rock Crusher" four-speed manual transmission.

The Goodwood Green coupe show here is one of the earliest L-88 Corvettes built, if not the earliest. Owned by noted collector Bill Tower, this curious machine exhibits more than one oddity that doesn't appear on other 1967 L-88s. Most noticeable are the "L/88" decals stuck on the hood and each valve cover. "An engineer at Chevrolet told me they were going to put these on the cars," recalls Tower, himself a former GM engineer. "They were going to use those decals, but they drew so much attention they decided against it. They didn't want just anyone buying an L-88, they didn't want everyone knowing about it."

That same logic came into play when Chevrolet officials grossly underrated the L-88 427 at 430 horsepower. "They used that number so that guys wanting the fastest Corvette available in 1967 would notice the 435-horse [L-71] engine instead," said Tower. "Again, they just wanted to sell the L-88 to real racers."

Eagle eyes might also notice the "wrong" Rally wheels with their deep-dish trim rings. Standard Sting Ray Rally rims in 1967 were 15x6 units with "skinny" trim rings. Like the decals on the hood,

MILESTONE FACTS

- L-88 Corvettes were built for three years. Production was 20 in 1967, 80 in 1968 and 116 in 1969.

- The L-88 was the first Corvette to use a functional hood scoop, this one pointed backward towards the cowl. Chevrolet engineers as far back as 1963 had discovered what tapping into the high-pressure area at the base of a car's windshield could do to free up a few more ponies on top end.

- Factory paperwork advised an L-88 buyer to steer clear of typical pump fuels: "This unit operates on Sunoco 260 or equivalent gas of very high octane. Under no circumstances should regular gasoline be used." Another label stuck inside the car repeated this warning. "Warning: vehicle must operate on a fuel having a minimum of 103 research octane and 95 motor octane or engine damage may result."

- Living with the optional J56 brakes in everyday operation was not easy. These fade-resistant clampers worked famously once warmed up. But when cold they were about as effective as Fred Flintstone's feet.

- Unlike the "stinger" hoods on typical big-block Corvettes in 1967, the L-88's lid was fully functional—it fed fresh air to the carb below.

- A transistorized ignition, RPO K66, was another mandatory L-88 option. The L-88 427 also used a mechanical-advance distributor.

- Special deep-groove pulleys were used on the L-88 427 to help prevent belts being thrown at high rpm.

Below left: *At Le Mans in June 1967 an L-88 topped 170 mph before a connecting rod disconnected.* **Above:** *Corvette chief engineer Zora Arkus-Duntov (on left) grins as engineer Denny Davis dyno tests an L-88 prototype in May 1966.*

the wheels on Tower's L-88 are experimental prototypes, and they're accordingly marked with "XP" identification. Measuring seven inches wide, they previewed the new rims introduced along with the restyled 1968 Corvette.

Anyone with eyes can see another "non-stock" feature: racing-style sidepipes. Originally manufactured by Stahl, these pipes and the full-race headers they're bolted to were also prototypes, in this case for the track-ready, wide-open exhausts that apparently were shipped in boxes to some L-88 Corvette buyers in 1967. Why all this special equipment?

Tower's car spent much of 1967 as a Proving Grounds testbed for the new L-88 package, during which time engineers thrashed everything from experimental high-speed Goodyear rubber to that functional fresh-air hood. Perhaps tested most thoroughly was the big Holley four-barrel, built specifically for the L-88 application. Holley engineer Marty Sullivan worked closely with GM people to

iron out early bugs and maximize performance with both differing exhaust setups and that new fresh-air hood. "That was part of my job, too," recalled Sullivan. "I worked along with the Chevy engineers who developed that scoop." "That hood wasn't just thrown together," added Tower. "They did a lot of testing to identify the flow characteristics of the air coming off the windshield."

When testing was finally done, Tower's green L-88 went south to Jim Rathmann's dealership in Melbourne, Florida, home to the handling of the complimentary Corvettes delivered to NASA astronauts. Indeed, the L-88 arrived in Melbourne on a hauler loaded with Sting Rays earmarked for the space program. Rathmann then sold the unique coupe to an old racing buddy, who later resold it in 1976 to Tower. Bill restored the rarity in 1995 after extensive research was performed to uncover its full background.

Is it the first L-88? He thinks so.

Left: These wheels are experimental prototypes measuring 15x7. Typical 1967 Corvette Rally wheels were 15x6 units.

Right: Feeding the 430-horse L-88 427 was a huge 850-cfm four-barrel carb specially prepared by Holley for this application.

L/88

Prototype "L/88" identification was created then cancelled to downplay the car's race-ready nature.

Chevrolet introduced the stunning Sting Ray coupe in 1963, and this body rolled on with minor updates up through 1967.

SPECIFICATIONS

Wheelbase: 98 inches

Weight: 3,200 pounds (approximate)

Original Price: $5,675

Engine: 427 cubic-inch L-88 V8 with aluminum cylinder heads

Compression: 12.5:1

Horsepower: 430 at 5,200 rpm

Induction: single 850-cfm Holley four-barrel carburetor on aluminum open-plenum manifold

Transmission: Muncie "Rock Crusher" (M-22) four-speed manual

Suspension: independent A-arms w/coil springs in front; independent with driveshafts acting as upper links, lower lateral links, trailing arms and transverse leaf spring

Brakes: power-assisted four-wheel discs

Production: 20 (coupes and convertibles)

1967 *Dodge* Charger 426 *Hemi*

"Four-twenty-six Hemi." What made the this big, bad hunk of Mopar muscle so special? Just ask any SS Chevelle or Cobra Jet Ford owner who dared cross paths with one back in the Sixties. Chrysler officials weren't lying when they said it produced 425 horses. Well, actually they were. In truth, output was higher than that.

Brute force was its forte. On top of that, the thing just looked so mean and nasty. Save perhaps for Ford's Boss 429, no other American performance powerplant looked like the 426 Hemi. And very few ran like it.

Chrysler Corporation had introduced its milestone hemi-head V8 in 1951, then dropped the design after 1958 in favor of lighter, equally powerful wedge-head V8s that were easier and cheaper to build. The concept then reappeared six years later, though in vastly different form. Based on Chrysler's 426 cubic-inch wedge V8, the '64 Hemi was an all-out competition engine never meant for the street.

The target was big Bill France's still-new superspeedway in Daytona Beach, Florida. In December 1962, engineer Tom Hoover had been asked to recreate the Hemi with the goal being to take it racing on the NASCAR circuit. Hoover's team then completed the

job just in time to for the sixth running of the Daytona 500 in February 1964, a race it dominated with ease. And that domination continued throughout the NASCAR season.

Chrysler's advantage was so great, Bill France decided—in the best interest of parity—to ban the Hemi in 1965. It was not a regular-production engine and thus was not legal to compete on his "stock car" circuit. Not ready to give up so easily, Chrysler officials then transformed the race Hemi into the street Hemi in 1966. By making the 426 Hemi a certified regular-production option, Chrysler then satisfied France's homologation requirements, and the Hemi was free to race again.

Taking the Hemi to the streets in 1966 required more than a little "detuning," beginning with a major compression cut. A less radical cam was stuffed in and the race Hemi's steel tube headers were replaced by cast-iron manifolds. On top, a heated aluminum intake mounting two Carter four-barrels superseded the exotic cross-ram manifold used previously.

The street Hemi was offered in a wide array of Dodge and Plymouth models from 1966 to '71. But if there was any one car that first year that best matched the Hemi's hot performance with equally hot looks it was Dodge's sleek, new Charger, a veritable stunner that turned heads with ease.

Introduced in January 1966, the Charger was, in Dodge general manager Byron Nichols' words, "a fresh new concept in styling and engineering excellence from bumper to bumper." Innocent by-standers, however, couldn't help but notice that the '66 Charger was not much more than a typical Coronet sedan with a trendy fastback roof tacked on. The two did share the same unit-body platform, with its 117-inch wheelbase, so the

Left: *Adding the optional 426 Hemi V8 to the Charger body in 1966 and '67 helped put the fast in fastback. Shown here is one of 118 Hemi Chargers built for 1967.*

MILESTONE FACTS

- Chrysler first reintroduced its hemi-head V8 in race-only form in 1964. A second "race Hemi" appeared in 1965, then the "street Hemi" was introduced in 1966.

- Counting the truly rare race-ready versions of 1964 and '65, Dodge and Plymouth rolled out roughly 10,500 Hemi cars during that eight-year run.

- The 426 Hemi first appeared as a Dodge Charger option in February 1966.

- "If you missed the San Francisco earthquake, reserve your seat here for a repeat performance," began a Car and Driver review of the 1966 street Hemi. "This automobile is the most powerful sedan ever, bar none."

- A standard interior feature in 1966, the Charger's large center console became an option in 1967.

- Total Charger production in 1967 was 15,788, compared to 37,300 for 1966.

- Hemi Charger production in 1966 was 468; 250 four-speeds, 218 automatics.

---

resemblance was certainly there. But not so fast. Based on the Charger II dream machine—a sleek, sexy sensation that began touring the auto show circuit in late 1964—the regular-production Charger represented an exceptional job of face-lifting a rather mundane model into and exciting fun machine.

V8 power was standard, beginning with a yeoman 318. At the top of the options list was 426 Hemi, which backed up all those fast looks with some serious performance. But all that muscle came at a price. The Hemi option alone ran in the $800 neighborhood. Throw in a long list of heavy-duty "mandatory options and the $3,100 base price began zooming towards five grand in a hurry, explaining why only 468 Hemi Chargers were sold in 1966.

Even fewer hit the streets in 1967. Minor Charger updates included new fender-mounted turn signals and an additional performance option, the 375-horse 440 cubic-inch big-block. Buyers who didn't mind the Hemi's cranky disposition and higher insurance costs could still opt for the 425-horse big-block, but only a handful did. Hemi Charger production in 1967 fell to 118.

The Hemi Charger returned in 1968, this time with yet another sleek, new body. Dodge built its last 425-horse Charger in 1971, after which time the Hemi was retired for good.

More than 10,000 "street Hemi" V8s were installed in Dodge and Plymouths from 1966 to 1971. Chrome-plated steel road wheels (lower left) were optional for Dodge's 1967 Charger. The first-generation Charger's unique interior (right) featured four bucket seats, with the rear pair folding down to increase usable storage space beneath that sloping rear window.

Beneath a 1967 Hemi's chrome air cleaner were two Carter four-barrel carburetors. Output was a conservatively rated 425 horsepower.

SPECIFICATIONS

Wheelbase: 117 inches

Weight: 4,160 pounds

Base Price: $4,500

Engine: 426 cubic-inch Hemi V8

Compression: 10.25:1

Horsepower: 425 at 5,000 rpm

Torque: 490 at 4,000 rpm

Induction: two 650-cfm Carter four-barrel carburetors

Transmission: four-speed manual with Hurst shifter

Suspension: independent A-arms w/torsion bars in front; live axle with leaf springs in back

Brakes: front discs, rear drums

Performance: 14.16 seconds at 96.15 mph in quarter-mile, according to Car Life magazine (test car equipped with Torqueflite automatic transmission)

Production: 59, with four-speed transmission—another 59 Hemi Chargers were built for 1967 with the Torqueflite automatic

1968 *Plymouth Road Runner*

Today the concept is known as the "biggest bang for the buck." This phrase, however, had yet to be coined in the fall of 1967 when Plymouth people woke up the masses with a musclecar that didn't require an arm and a leg to own.

By 1967 performance models were by no means collecting dust in showrooms, but more and more were becoming E-ticket rides. That year there were many factory hot rods priced above $3,300 that could reach 100 mph in the quarter-mile. Yet not one below that bottom line could score triple digits. Thus became Plymouth's "frugal" goal for 1968: "100 mph in the quarter for less than $3,000.

To meet this end Plymouth designers kept non-essentials to a minimum. A bare-bones Belvedere sedan, with swing-out rear windows instead of roll-up units, was initially chosen as the foundation for the project. That foundation was then typically beefed up with stiffened suspension components and F70 wide-tread rubber mounted on wide steel rims adorned only with low-buck "dog-dish" hubcaps. Inside, the basic interior was as spartan as a taxi-cab save for that tall, shiny floor shifter. As expected, a four-speed manual gearbox was standard—no wimpy column-shifted three-speed here. Image-conscious bucket seats were not

Below: *Plymouth did right by licensing the Road Runner cartoon image from Warner Brothers for its "mass-market" musclecar, one of the Sixties' best-remembered factory hot rods.*

offered, and frivolity was limited to a blacked-out grille, a GTX hood, a couple of decals printed up with Warner Brothers' express permission, and that cute "beep-beep" horn. "Road Runner" was the name; speeding away from wily Goats was the game.

Customers of all ages loved every bit of it: the name, the horn and the nicely affordable musclecar behind it all. By paying attention were it mattered most, Plymouth designers were able to keep the Road Runner's base price at roughly $2,900—and without skimping on the muscle. Beneath the hood was a clever combination of passenger-car power source and hot-ticket hardware. The Road Runner's standard 383 cubic-inch V8 shared cylinder heads, crankcase windage tray, intake manifold and cam with the big-bully 375-horse 440. With next to no muss and very little fuss, Plymouth engineers had produced a relatively cheap performance V8 able to make 335 horses on command, and that power fit the original plan nicely.

"Plymouth figures, and rightly so, that one way to win you over this year is to give you lots of car for your money," raved a February 1968 Car Life review. "In the case of the Road Runner, Plymouth's idea is to give lots of performance for the money, and it does this partly by putting gobs of go-goodies into the car, partly by not charging tremendous amounts for it, and partly by keeping things simple."

Calling the new Road Runner "the world's fastest club coupe," the Car and Driver test crew pointed out that "this is the first car since the GTO to be aimed directly at American youth and it very probably is dead on target. But just wait till ol' Nader hears about it."

Fortunately American youth got wind of the Road Runner before Ralph (he wasn't that old then) and his consumer-conscious "Raiders" got a chance to spoil things. Demand for Plymouth's mainstream musclecar quickly skyrocketed with 1968 production reaching 44,599. Within a year the Road Runner was America's second best-selling musclecar behind (by only a few grand) the new leader, Chevy's SS 396 Chevelle. The former front-runner, Pontiac's GTO, ranked a distant third.

Clearly Plymouth had proven that less indeed could be more. Maybe so, but not all early Road Runners were low-buck bombs. Options were typically plentiful, and most prominent on the extra-cost shelf was the always-awesome 426 Hemi.

Talk about a budget-buster. The '68 Road Runner's only optional power source, the Hemi wore a hefty price tag of $715, and the bottom-line beating didn't stop there. Adding those 425 horses into the mix also meant the mandatory installation (for four-speed cars; it was optional with the Torqueflite automatic) of the

MILESTONE FACTS

- Plymouth introduced the Road Runner in 1968 and continued building it up through 1975.

- Total production in 1968 was 44,599—29,240 coupes and 15,359 hardtops.

- Adding to the Road Runner image was a horn that went "beep-beep" just like the cartoon character.

- Advertisements even referring to Plymouth's new musclecar species by its Latin name, "acceleratii rapidus maximus."

- Enough changes were made to the 426 Hemi in 1968 to earn the designation "Stage II." A slightly hotter cam and recalibrated carbs were the main revamps. Compression remained at 10.25:1 and output stayed at 425 horsepower.

- Domestic production of Hemi Road Runners in 1968 was 840 coupes and 169 hardtops. Of those coupes, 449 had four-speeds, 391 had automatics. The breakdown for the Hemi hardtops read 108 four-speeds, 61 automatics.

- An A833 four-speed manual transmission was standard for the '68 Road Runner. The Torqueflite automatic was optional.

- A Road Runner convertible was offered in 1969 for one year only.

- Motor Trend magazine named the 1969 Road Runner its "Car of the Year."

- Road Runner sales in 1969 soared to 84,420, second only by a couple grand to the muscle market leader, Chevy's '69 SS 396—and about 12,000 more than the former king, Pontiac's GTO.

heavy-duty Dana 60 rearend with Sure-Grip differential and 3.54:1 gears, a package priced at $139. All Hemi Road Runners were also fitted with their own special K-member subframe and further-stiffened suspension, improved cooling, heavy-duty drum brakes, and big 15-inch wheels and tires.

Though it defeated the whole budget-minded purpose, mating high-rolling Hemi power with the plain-Jane Road Runner resulted in a predictably fast automobile. Low 13s were no problem, leading Motor Trend's resident muscle maven, Eric Dahlquist, to label the sum of the parts "probably the fastest production sedan made today."

On the flipside, the cost of all this earth-shaking speed was nearly $4,400, a figure well out of Average Joe's reach in 1968. But if you had the dough and the desire, could you name a better buy? Who cared about "biggest bang for the buck" when a Hemi offered the biggest bang, period?

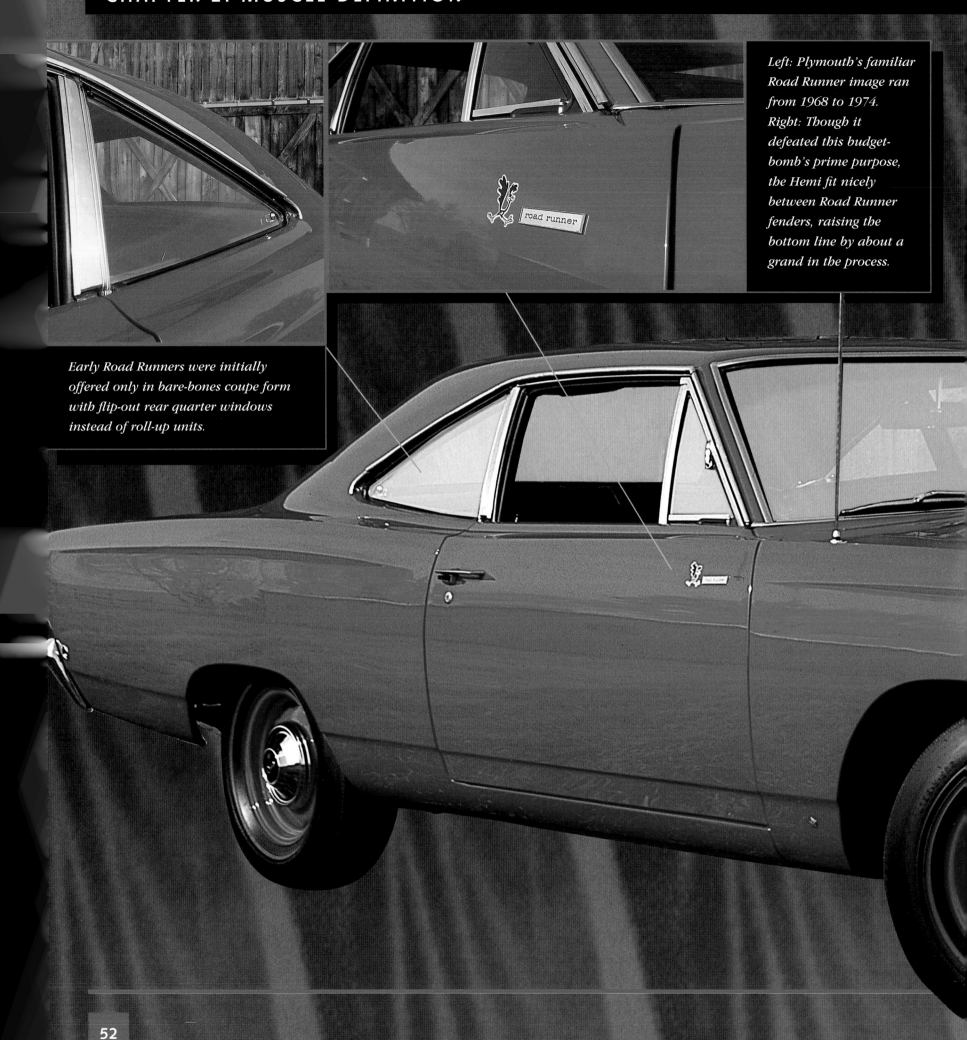

Left: Plymouth's familiar Road Runner image ran from 1968 to 1974. Right: Though it defeated this budget-bomb's prime purpose, the Hemi fit nicely between Road Runner fenders, raising the bottom line by about a grand in the process.

Early Road Runners were initially offered only in bare-bones coupe form with flip-out rear quarter windows instead of roll-up units.

1968 Road Runners were powered by either the standard 383 V8 or the optional 426 Hemi.

SPECIFICATIONS

Wheelbase: 116 inches

Weight: 3,880 pounds

Original price: $4,400

Engine: 426 cubic-inch Hemi V8

Compression: 10.25:1

Horsepower: 425 at 5,000 rpm

Torque: 490 at 4,000 rpm

Induction: two Carter AFB four-barrel carburetors

Transmission: three-speed Torqueflite automatic

Suspension: independent A-arms w/torsion bars in front; live axle with leaf springs in back

Brakes: front discs, rear drums

Production (coupe w/Hemi V8): 840; 449 with four-speeds, 391 with automatics

1968-½ Ford Mustang 428 CJ

Three years after Ford kicked off Detroit's ponycar race with a bang in April 1964, Dearborn officials found themselves choking on dust as rival copies of their wildly popular Mustang began galloping away with the burgeoning performance car market.

Introduced for 1967, GM's F-body Camaro and Firebird both offered loads of ponycar pizzazz, as well as optional big-block power. In response, Ford designers fattened the second-generation Mustang to make room for its own big-block, but the '67 GT with its 390-cube FE-series V8 was no match for Chevy's SS 396 Camaro and Pontiac's Firebird 400.

Leave it to Robert F. Tasca. Credited with originating the phrase, "win on Sunday, sell on Monday," Tasca was no stranger to Ford performance, having promoted it openly from his East Providence,

Rhode Island, dealership since 1961. First came sponsorship of a locally successful 1962 406 Galaxie, followed by a full-fledged drag race team that scored NHRA Winternationals championships in 1964 and '65. By then, Tasca Ford had established itself as the mecca in the East for Blue-Oval performance followers. If it was hot, it was on Tasca's lot at 777 Taunton Avenue.

Below: *One of 50 specially prepared lightweight Cobra Jet Mustangs warms up at Pomona prior to the NHRA Winternationals in 1968.*

Yet, despite great success as a speed merchant, not even Bob "The Bopper" Tasca could teach a new dog old tricks, a task put before him as the supposedly strong '67 Mustang GTS began rolling onto his lot from Ford. As Tasca's performance manager, Dean Gregson, told Hot Rod's Eric Dahlquist, "we found the [390 Mustang] so non-competitive, we began to feel we were cheating the customer. We had to do something."

Actually the solution came about much by luck after a Tasca employee trashed the 390 FE in a '67 GT coupe while street racing. In place of the grenaded 390 went a 428 Police Interceptor short-block wearing reworked heads and a 735-cfm Holley four-barrel, equipment that instantly transformed the car into a 13-second quarter-mile killer.

MILESTONE FACTS

- Ford offered the 428 Cobra Jet as a mid-year "1968-1/2" option for Fairlanes, Torinos, Cougars and mid-sized Mercurys, but the CJ garnered the most attention as the brave new heart of a new, truly muscular Mustang.

- CJ Mustang production commenced at the Dearborn assembly plant on December 13, 1967. First came at least 50 specially prepared fastbacks: lightweight, strip-ready super-stock Mustangs with all sealers and sound deadeners deleted. These models, all painted Wimbledon White, were built for one job: to promote Ford's newest breed of ponycar performance at the drags.

- Regular production of street-going CJ Mustangs began after the run of super-stock drag cars was completed. Dealers received notice of the 428 Cobra Jet engine option on March 29, 1968. Its price was $420.

- The CJ Mustang Eric Dahlquist tested for Hot Rod was probably one of those first 50 super stock specials. Dahlquist does remember it lacking sealer and sound deadener.

- A team of white Cobra Jet Mustangs showed up in Pomona, California, for the NHRA Winternationals in 1968, and Al Joniec's CJ took top Super/Stock honors with a run of 12.12 seconds at 109.48 mph.

- A Car Craft track test of a super-stock Mustang CJ, driven by Dyno Don Nicholson and Hubert Platt, pushed the envelope even further to 11.62 seconds at 119.7 mph. To that Car Craft's John Raffa wrote that "Ford's new 428 Cobra Jet Mustang Super/Stocker can best be described as a car with hair!"

- The 335-horse 428 Cobra Jet remained a Mustang option up through 1970

- The 428 CJ became the Fairlane Cobra's standard powerplant in 1969.

Called the "KR," for "King of the Road," Tasca's 428 Mustang inspired Hot Rod's Dahlquist to ask his readers if Ford should built a regular-production version. Once a few thousand positive responses began piling up on Henry Ford II's desk, Dearborn designers got the hint.

Following Tasca's lead, Ford engineers simply mixed and matched a collection of existing FE-series big-block parts. Using a 428 passenger-car block as a base, they added 427 low-riser heads and a cast-iron version of Ford's aluminum Police Interceptor (PI) intake mounting Tascas's big 735 Holley. A 390 GT cam, PI rods, and 10.6:1 pistons went inside, while low-restriction dual exhausts completed the package, which debuted on April 1, 1968.

Passing on Tasca's suggested name, Ford's braintrust instead chose the "Cobra Jet" moniker for the hot new 335-horse 428, leaving Carroll Shelby to pick up on the KR label for his CJ-powered GT500 Mustang. Who was the mastermind behind the Cobra Jet label? It was more or less a team effort.

"We already had the snake idea in our heads," explained Ford engineer Bill Barr. "And we didn't do this like we normally did. We didn't just roll out the product with everyone standing around it scratching their asses trying to name it. The idea was already rolling by then. Some artist in Styling had already created a drawing of the Cobra emblem—the snake and the wheels and exhausts coming out of its tale. We had the drawing, then the name came from there."

Offered in fastback, coupe and convertible forms, the CJ Mustang also featured a long list of standard performance pieces, including power front discs, braced shock towers, a beefy 9-inch rearend, staggered rear shocks (on four-speed models), and a black-striped ram-air hood. An 8000-rpm tach was standard with the four-speed, optional when a C6 automatic transmission was chosen. Part of the deal, too, was the GT equipment group consisting of a heavy-duty suspension, F70 tires on styled-steel wheels, fog lamps, chromed quad exhaust tips, and "GT" identification.

Testing a specially prepared Cobra Jet prototype, Hot Rod reported a sensational 13.56-second quarter-mile time. Thoroughly impressed, Eric Dahlquist concluded that "the CJ will be the utter delight of every Ford lover and the bane of all the rest because, quite frankly, it is probably the fastest regular-production sedan ever built."

It was also the car responsible for saving Ford's bacon in the great American musclecar race.

Left: All Cobra Jets in 1968 were GT models, meaning they wore bright styled-steel wheels with trim rings and "GT" center caps. Right: Also among standard GT equipment was a competition-style flip-open gas cap.

Right: Ford's first Cobra Jet Mustang was offered with either a four-speed manual or Cruise-O-Matic automatic transmission. Far right: The striped hood scoop was fully functional. Ram-air was standard.

SPECIFICATIONS

Wheelbase: 108 inches

Weight: 3,623 pounds

Original price: $3,600, approximate

Engine: 428 cubic-inch Cobra Jet V8

Compression: 10.6:1

Induction: single 735-cfm Holley four-barrel carburetor

Horsepower: 335 at 5,600 rpm

Torque: 440 at 3,400 rpm

Transmission: four-speed manual

Suspension: independent A-arms w/coil springs in front; live axle with leaf springs and staggered shocks in back in back

Brakes: power front discs, rear drums

Performance: 13.56 seconds in the quarter-mile, according to Hot Rod

Production: 2,827 (2,253 fastbacks, 564 hardtops, and 10 convertibles)

1969 Chevelle SS 396

In the beginning Chevrolet's legendary SS 396 Chevelle was a little-known, limited-edition teaser created to test the market waters that Pontiac had first splashed head-long into with its GTO in 1964. Only 201 "Z16" Malibu Super Sports were built in 1965, all fully loaded, and all wearing a price tag that would wilt the wallet of most musclecar fanatics.

With Chevrolet's new 396 cubic-inch Mk IV big-block leading the way atop a long list of standard performance and prestige features, the Z16 Malibu cost about $4,200, compared to $2,590 for a base small-block Chevelle. Most of those Z16s went to celebrities and prominent press people, all in the best interests of kicking off a high-powered bloodline with a high-profile bang.

When it returned in 1966, the SS 396 Chevelle was less potent in standard form, but was also less costly, all in the best interests of

appealing to a mass audience. Although it was still based on the Malibu sport coupe (or convertible), it used a more civilized 325-horsepower 396 for standard power in place of the Z16's truly potent 375-horse Mk IV V8. This power reduction, combined with the deletion of many of the Z16's standard feature, resulted in a

Below: *Chevrolet's popular SS 396 Chevelle unseated Pontiac's GTO as America's best-selling musclecar in 1969.*

more palatable base price of $2,776 for the '66 SS 396. This in turn resulted in sales of 72,000 Super Sport Chevelles that year. If a customer wanted Z16-type performance, all he had to do was ante up for various appropriate options, topped by RPO L78, the 375-horse 396.

By 1969, the popular SS 396 Chevelle had screamed past Pontiac's GTO to become Detroit's best-selling musclecar. Total production for all SS 396 varieties in 1969 hit 86,307, compared to 72,287 for Pontiac's "Goat."

In other news for 1969, Chevrolet changed the way it offered the SS 396 to power-hungry customers. In 1968, the SS 396 model lines included a Malibu sport coupe, convertible and El Camino. Beginning the following year, an SS 396 buyer had to check off RPO Z25, which was offered for those same three bodystyles, plus two new ones in the low-priced 300 series. Both the 300 Deluxe sport coupe and 300 Deluxe sedan could have been transformed into an SS 396 in 1969, the only year a Super Sport Chevelle could have been anything other than a top-of-the-line Malibu or Custom El Camino.

Priced at $347.60, RPO Z25 was basically the same SS 396 package offered from 1966 to '68, with a couple of nice additions thrown in for good measure. Standard power still came from the 325-hose 396 backed by a three-speed manual, and a beefed-up chassis remained as well. On top, the SS hood with its twin bulges carried over, as did the blackout treatment for the grille and rear cove panel. "SS 396" badging once more graced both ends. Inside, the standard benchseat interior again featured "SS" identification on the steering wheel and "SS 396" tags on both the door panels and the dashboard's passenger side—actually, the dashboard emblem read "Super Sport" in 1966 and '67.

On the outside, the '69 Super Sport received new "SS 396" emblems on the fenders. And the deletion of all the excess lower body clutter used in 1968 (contrasting black paint, chrome trim delineation, various stripe treatments) helped clean things up considerably. A customer could add the contrasting lower-body paint at extra cost, but the standard scheme looked attractive enough without it. A more suitable choice was the D96 wide upper-body accent stripe.

MILESTONE FACTS

- Introduced in limited-fashion in 1965, the SS 396 Chevelle eventually rose up in 1969 to unseat Pontiac's GTO as this country's best-selling musclecar.

- Late in 1969 the 396 cubic-inch V8 was bored out to 402 cubes. The name, however, remained "SS 396."

- For one year only, 1969, a Chevy customer could've ordered an SS 396 sedan. That year the Super Sport package became an option package, RPO Z25, available for Malibu sports coupes and convertible, Custom El Caminos, and 300 Deluxe coupes and sedans. All other SS 396s (save, of course, for the convertible and El Camino variety) built on other years were based on the Malibu sports coupe.

- The SS 396's base engine in 1969 was the 325-horse L35 396. Next on the options list was a 350-hp 396, RPO L34. At the top was the 375-horse L78.

- About 300 Chevelles were equipped with the Corvette's 425-horse L72 427 V8 in 1969 by way of the clandestine COPO paperwork.

- Chevrolet introduced the L89 aluminum-head option for the Chevelle Super Sport's L78 396 only in 1969. These heads did not change the L78's 375-horse-rating; the idea was to shave off unwanted pounds from the potent big-block. L89/L78 production in 1969 was 400.

- Two radioactive Camaro paint choices were offered to SS 396 buyers in 1969: Hugger Orange and Daytona Yellow. Applying either shade added an extra $42.15 to the bottom line.

The most prominent additions to the SS 396 standard equipment list in 1969 were power front disc brakes and a set of new five-spoke SS wheels. The former used 11-inch rotors and single-piston calipers. The latter featured small "SS" center caps and bright trim rings. Set off by chrome wheel opening moldings, these sporty 14x7 rims were the only wheels available for the '69 SS 396 and represented a marked departure from the "dog-dish" hubcaps that had been standard from 1966 to '68.

A nicely well-rounded package inside and out, the Chevrolet's SS 396 deserved its place as America's number-one musclecar in 1969. And the Super Sport Chevelle remained in the lead right up to the end in the Seventies. Did it get any better? Ask the man who owned one, like Fred Koss, of Pesotum, Illinois. He bought the red SS 396 shown here new in 1969—and still owns it today.

When you own the best, why give it up?

Far left: Snazzy five-spoke sport wheels became standard SS 396 equipment in 1969. Typical steel rims with hubcaps had been standard from 1966 to 1968.

Left: An attractive sport steering wheel was one of many interior options for the 1969 SS 396. Full instrumentation, buckets seats and a console were also offered.

Chevrolet kicked off its SS 396 Chevelle legacy in 1965. This familiar badge last appeared in 1970.

A 325-horsepower 396 was standard for the 1969 SS 396. Options included a 350-horse big-block and the top-shelf L78 V8 (shown here), rated at 375 horses.

SPECIFICATIONS

Wheelbase: 112 inches

Weight: 3,900 pounds

Base Price: RPO Z25, the SS 396 package, added $347.60 to the base sticker ($2,673)'69 Malibu sport coupe.

Engine: 396 cubic-inch L-78 V8

Compression: 11.0:1

Horsepower: 375 at 5,600 rpm

Torque: 415 at 3,600 rpm

Induction: single Holley four-barrel carburetor

Transmission: Turbo Hydramatic automatic

Suspension: independent A-arms w/coil springs in front; live axle with coil springs in back

Brakes: front discs, rear drums

Production: 9,486 w/L78 396 (for both SS 396 and El Camino SS 396)

1969 *AMC Hurst* SC/Rambler

Born in 1954 after the merger of veteran independents Nash and Hudson, American Motors Corporation seemingly always was off in its own world out there in Kenosha, Wisconsin. Affordable, economical, albeit bland transportation quickly became AMC's forte, and this main selling point proved to be just the ticket once money got tight around American households during the late Fifties.

Sales soared in 1959 and remained strong for a few more years. In 1963 Motor Trend magazine even named American Motors' compact Rambler its "Car of the Year." Then reality set in. AMC cars were dull and boring, while the Sixties scene was hip and happening. What was a Detroit outsider to do?

Why not jump up onto the musclecar bandwagon? After some serious down times, AMC did just that, though a bit hesitantly at first. In 1967 the company became the last automaker to finally denounce the infamous AMA anti-racing edict of 1957, then followed that up with two all-new, all-exciting cars—the sporty Javelin and hot, little AMX two-seater—in 1968. But that was only

the beginning. In 1969, with the help of the Hurst Performance people, the Kenosha company rolled out an outrageous super-stock Javelin equipped to go right to the dragstrip. Only about 50 of these red-white-and-blue factory race cars were built that year, with not one ever intended for daily driving chores.

More sociably acceptable was a second factory hot rod created in 1969 through cooperation between AMC and Hurst. Based on American Motors' diminutive Rogue coupe, the Hurst SC/Rambler was one of the flashiest fun machines ever let loose during the original musclecar era. In keeping with American Motors' established tradition, the car was done up in a patriotic finish that didn't have to beg anyone to take a look. On top of basic white paint went large red accent panels down each bodyside and a blue stripe up over the top. The wheel centers, too, were blue, as was the big "arrow" on the hood that directed air into a somewhat odd, boxy scoop. For those who weren't sure what was going on, that scoop was appropriately labeled with red "AIR" lettering, and the arrow identified the engine that was sucking that atmosphere in: AMC's "390 cu. in." V8.

The first 500 SC/Ramblers built for 1969 all were done up in that same image. The next 500 off the line, however, were toned down by leaving off the red bodyside accents. The final 512 then appeared looking just like the first group. AMC enthusiasts today know those 1,012

Left and opposite page: *Two exteriors were offered for the SC/Rambler, the type A with its red bodysides (at left) and the type B with its bare white panels (far right).*

cars with their red sides as "Type A" models. The other 500 without the red are, you guessed it, "Type B's."

Either way, A or B, the '69 Hurst SC/Rambler also represented one of the best buys from high-performance days gone by. Its base sticker was just short of $3,000, and that wasn't a stripped-down price for a stripped-down car. Standard equipment included a Borg-Warner T-10 close-ratio four-speed manual transmission with a Hurst shifter, a 10.5-inch clutch, power front disc brakes, a heavy-duty cooling package, a suitably beefed suspension, and a Twin Grip differential containing 3.54:1 gears. That stout suspension consisted of typically stiffened springs and shocks, a thickened front sway bar, and rear axle torque links to help prevent spring windup and wheel hop during hard acceleration.

Inside were bucket seats, a sport steering wheel, and a Sun tachometer

MILESTONE FACTS

• Hurst and AMC announced the SC/Rambler on February 13, 1969. The car then debuted at the Chicago Auto Show in March.

• "Well imagine the looks on the faces when you lay down an e.t. in the low 14s at say, 98 mph… right off the showroom floor!," read an AMC press release detailing the SC/Rambler. "And set it up for the strip with a little sharp tuning, who knows? You might be turning 12s."

• The 315-horse 390 V8 breathed through a vacuum-activated ram-air hood scoop. On the other end was a unique dual exhaust system fitted with "Special-Tone" mufflers and chrome tips in back.

• The SC/Rambler's standard heavy-duty cooling package included a high-capacity radiator and a "Power-Flex" fan with shroud. Those flexible fan blades automatically decreased in pitch at higher speeds to save power and reduce noise.

• Tires were E70 Goodyear Polyglas Wide-Treads adorned with trendy red stripes.

strapped to the steering column. Along with all that pizzazz on the outside were dual racing mirrors, racing style hood tie-down pins and 14x6 five-spoke sport wheels.

The real star of the show, though, came beneath that functional boxy scoop. Fed by a Carter four-barrel carb, AMC's 390-cube V8 produced 315 horses. Combine that power with roughly 3,100 pounds of lightweight Rogue and the results were predictable—the SC/Rambler could indeed run the quarter in roughly 14 seconds. A dip or two into AMC's hot parts bin could quicken that pace up in a heartbeat.

Yet as hot as the SC/Rambler was, it didn't quite attract the following AMC officials had hoped. Many critics loved its performance, but pooh-poohed all that "American-way" frivolity. Thus, the car ended up a one-hit wonder.

AMC designers, however, just couldn't leave well enough alone. They came back in 1970 with their Rebel Machine, another red-white-and-blue screamer wearing a boxy hood scoop—and yet another American Motors musclecar all but lost in the shadows of horsepower history.

SPECIFICATIONS

Wheelbase: 106 inches

Weight: 3,160 pounds

Base Price: $2,998

Engine: 390 cubic-inch V8

Compression: 10.2:1

Induction: single Carter four-barrel carburetor with ram-air hood scoop

Horsepower: 315 at 4,600 rpm

Torque: 425 at 3,200 rpm

Transmission: Hurst-shifted Borg-Warner t-10 four-speed manual

Suspension: independent A-arms w/coil springs in front; live axle with leaf springs in back

Brakes: power front discs, rear drums

Performance: 14.14 seconds at 100.9 mph in the quarter-mile, according to Road & Track

Production: 1,512

Patriotic paint carried over to the SC/Rambler's wheels (left). The Hurst shifter people teamed up with various automakers, including AMC in 1969 (right).

A tachometer, strapped to the steering column in street-racer fashion, was including in the SC/Rambler deal.

It was boxy and odd-looking, but this hood scoop did ram cooler, denser outside air into the carb below.

1970 *Buick* GSX Stage 1

General Motors dominated the early supercar race with Pontiac's GTO and Oldsmobile's 4-4-2 kicking things off in 1964. In 1965 Buick followed that lead with the first of its long-running Gran Sports, a classy machine based on the division's mid-sized Skylark model.

Born in Flint, Michigan, where "better cars" were built, Buick's gentlemanly GS, in the opinion of Car Life magazine's editors, came "off stronger, more distinctive [than its GM cousins] and with something its owners can appreciate"—that being a humble asking price. Priced at a tidy $200, the GS option added a 325-horse 401-cube V8, a beefier convertible frame, and those ever-present heavy-duty chassis upgrades.

But don't kid yourself. Just because it was a Buick didn't mean a Gran Sport's appeal was totally intended for gentlemen. Performance escalations in Flint during the Sixties included the 1969 introduction of the division's revered "Stage 1" engine package, offered that first year for the firm's 400 cubic-inch big-block V8. Among other things, Stage 1 parts included a hotter cam and a modified Rochester Quadra-Jet four-barrel carburetor topped with a ram-air hood. Output for the Stage 1 400 was a laughable 350 horses, though few got the joke. Not many muscleheads took Buick performance seriously, so even the super-strong Stage 1 was commonly overlooked—that is, until it left an unsuspecting victim eating dust at a traffic light. "If the [Stage 1 Buick] had a GTO sheetmetal wrapper on it," wrote Hot Rod's Steve Kelley, "you couldn't build enough of 'em."

MILESTONE FACTS

- Total Buick Gran Sport production in 1970 was 20,096. Of these, 9,948 were powered by 350-cid small-block V8s. Buick also built 1,416 GS convertibles that year, all with 455-cid big-blocks.

- All GSX Buicks were hardtops. Total GSX production for 1970 was 678, followed by 124 in 1971.

- Buick's Stage 1 455 Gran Sport was one of the last Seventies musclecars standing around Detroit. It was still in the scene in 1974.

- Like Oldmobile's 4-4-2, Buick's Gran Sport was treated to a 455 cubic-inch big-block V8 in 1970 after General Motors dropped its 400-cid limit for its mid-sized model lines.

- Buick parts books also listed even more outrageous "Stage 2" components for its big-block V8s. Yet as potent as these parts were, they garnered little attention 30-odd years back. Even fewer horsepower hounds recall them today.

Token Stage 1 output went up 10 horses in 1970 as cubic inches for Buick's biggest big-block zoomed to 455. After watching a 455 Stage 1 Gran Sport scorch the quarter-mile in a scant 13.38 seconds, Motor Trend's Bill Sanders called this ground-shaking Buick an "old man's car inbred with a going street bomb." Continued Sanders, "It may be some vague sort of incest, but the results are pretty exciting. Performance verges on a precipitous mechanical hysteria. The first time you put your foot to the boards a premonition of impending whiplash emanates from the base of the Achilles tendon."

Exciting words indeed. And this was before Buick designers started dressing up their Stage 1 455 in a shocking sheetmetal wrapper the likes of which performance buyers had never seen before. On February 9, 1970, Buick introduced its gonzo-looking GSX at the Chicago Auto Show. Along with a hot suspension, 15x7 sport wheels shod in fat G60 Goodyear Polyglas GT rubber, and power front disc brakes, the GSX featured what may well rank as the musclecar era's highest profile image treatment.

Included were front and rear spoilers, color-coordinated headlight bezels (standard GS units were chromed), black bodyside accent stripes and twin black hood stripes (all trimmed in red pinstriping), a hood-mounted tachometer, dual racing mirrors and "GSX" identification. Accompanying all this was either Apollo White or Saturn Yellow paint. Inside, black was the only available shade. Bucket seats, a consolette, a Rallye steering wheel, gauges and a Rallye clock were also present and accounted for.

Beneath that bodacious skin was Buick's Rally Ride Control Package, consisting of heavy-duty front (1-inch) and rear (0.875-inch) sway bars, boxed lower control arms and performance-tuned springs and shocks. Standard power came from a 350-horsepower 455 big-block backed by a four-speed and a limited-slip differential carrying 3.42:1 gears in back. The sum of these parts, identified by Buick options code "A9," added roughly $1,100 to a Gran Sport's bottom line in 1970.

For those with a little pocket change left over there were some interesting options, the foremost being the fabled Stage 1 V8. Beneath a yellow or white GSX hood, the Stage 1 option was priced at $113 in 1970. It cost $199 when ordered for a "typical" GS. But unlike the GS Stage 1, the GSX version carried no exterior identification, meaning most challengers on the street never even knew what hit them.

Also on the extra-cost list was the three-speed Turbo Hydramatic 400 automatic. Like the Stage 1 option, the TH 400 cost far less (442.14) in a GSX than in a GS. That may explain why 409 of the 678 GSX buyers chose the TH 400 automatic in 1970. Of those 409, 289 were Stage 1 cars; the remaining 120 were paired up with the 350-horse 455.

Buick rolled out a second-edition GSX in 1971 before all that flashy fun came to a halt. A less-prominent GSX option was offered in 1972, and both the Gran Sport and the Stage 1 455 carried on for a few more years afterward, but without all that extra pizzazz on the outside. The GSX's radioactive glow, however, is still remembered today.

Opposite page: *Either gleaming Apollo White and snazzy Saturn Yellow paint adorned the GSX in 1970. No exterior engine identification was included.*

Above: *Buick's Gran Sport first appeared in 1965 as a "gentleman's hot rod" of sorts. There was nothing gentle about the new GSX in 1970.*

SPECIFICATIONS

Wheelbase: 112 inches

Weight: 3,920 pounds

Base Price: $3,700

Engine: 455 cubic-inch Stage 1 V8

Induction: single Rochester Quadrajet four-barrel carburetor

Compression: 10.5:1

Horsepower: 360 at 4,600 rpm

Torque: 510 at 2,800 rpm

Transmission: Turbo Hydramatic automatic

Suspension: independent A-arms w/coil springs in front; four-link live axle with coil springs in back

Brakes: power front discs, rear drums

Performance: 13.95 seconds at 100.50 mph for the quarter-mile

Production (w/Stage 1 455 V8): 400

Buick's Stage 1 455 V8 was optional for the GSX; the hood-mounted tach (right) was standard.

"GSX" identification appeared in the grille, on the rear quarters (opposite page lower left), and on the rear spoiler's trailing edge (right).

GSX

Fat Goodyear rubber on 15x7 sport wheels was standard for the GSX.

1967 *Chevy* Z/28 CAMARO

Introduced to the automotive press on November 26, 1966, at Riverside, California, Chevrolet's first Z/28 was nothing more than a street-going extension of Chevy's Sports Car Club of America racing effort. Initiated in 1966, the SCCA's Tran-Am sedan series had ended up being a one-horse show in its first year as Ford's Mustang took all the marbles running against a pack of Plymouth Barracudas and Dodge Darts.

And things almost ended right then and there—apparently race fans weren't too keen on watching Mustangs beat up on Barracuda and Darts all day long. Not until Chevrolet's Vince Piggins convinced SCCA officials that his company would honor Trans-Am competition with its presence did a 1967 race schedule become reality.

On August 17, 1966, Piggins, then an assistant staff engineer in charge of performance product promotion, issued a memo to upper brass outlining his plan to build an SCCA-legal factory racer based on Chevrolet's new ponycar, the Camaro. Once approved, Piggins' proposed package was given regular production order (RPO) number Z28, a label that stuck despite Vince's pleas for the name "Cheetah."

To meet SCCA homologation standards, the officially named "Z/28" had to have a back seat (which made it a "sedan"), it had to have a wheelbase no longer than 116 inches, it had to have an engine no larger than 305 cubes, and it had to sold to the public no less than 1,000 times. The first two requirements were no problem, and the production quota scared no one at Chevrolet—"the sales department anticipates a volume of 10,000 such vehicles [for] 1967," wrote Piggins in his August 17 memo. It was the engine size limit that presented the real challenge.

Below: *Chevrolet's Z/28 Camaro debuted somewhat quietly in 1967. "Z/28" fender badges didn't appear until 1968.*

A truly hot 302 cubic-inch small-block V8 was created exclusively for the Z/28 Camaro by stuffing a 283 crank into a 327 to stay within the 305-cid maximum. Though the cylinder block was a typical passenger-car unit with two-bolt main bearings (stronger four-bolt mains came along in 1969), the rugged crank was made of forged steel instead of nodular cast-iron. L79 big-port heads, 11:1 pistons, a radical solid-lifter cam, and an 800-cfm Holley four-barrel carb on an aluminum intake heated things up further. Advertised output was 290 horses. Seat-of-the-pants readings, however, went much higher, some as lofty as 400 horsepower.

Whatever the true number, the 302 impressed the press to no end. "The very-backdoor word is that [destroking the 327] has resulted in a happy and extremely potent screamer," wrote Sports Car Graphic's Jerry Titus, while Car and Driver simply labeled the 302 the "most responsive American V8s we've ever tested." That was big talk for a small-block.

Deserving of similar raves was the 302's supporting cast. Per Piggins' original plan, Chevrolet's superb F41 sports suspension was included as part of RPO Z28. So was a quick-ratio Saginaw manual steering box and 3.73:1 rear gears. A Muncie four-speed transmission with a 2.20:1 low was a mandatory option, as were RPO's J56 and J52—front disc brakes and power assist, respectively. Thrown in along with those discs were four smart-looking 15x6 Corvette Rally wheels. Other than these bright rims, the only other outward sign of a '67 Z/28's presence were twin racing stripes on the hood and rear deck. The legendary "Z/28" emblem didn't debut until midway through 1968.

MILESTONE FACTS

- Chevrolet's first Trans-Am ponycar carried no external identification. Those legendary "Z/28" badges didn't show up until 1968.

- Included as Z/28 standard equipment in 1967, the F41 suspension consisted of heavy-duty springs, stiff shocks, and a radius rod on the axle's right side to control wheel hop.

- An optional cowl-induction air-cleaner was shipped in the trunk of some '67 Z/28 Camaros. Headers too were offered, but few were sold.

- Z/28 production soared to 7,199 in 1968, then topped 19,000 the following year.

- Chevy's Z/28 legacy was briefly interrupted in 1975 and '76. Returning in 1977, the hot-to-trot Camaro remained popular into the new millennium.

- In 1970 the Z/28 received a stunning new body and a new engine based on the Corvette's LT-1 350 small-block.

In all, only 602 Z/28 Camaros were built in 1967. How then did Chevrolet take it racing on the Trans-Am circuit? Officials played a little numbers game by homologating the 350-cid Camaro—which darn near grew on trees compared to the Z/28—under Federation Internationale de l'Automobile (FIA, the world governing body over SCCA racing) Group I rules, then qualified that car equipped with RPO Z28 under Group II specifications. Don't understand? Don't worry, neither did the competition back in 1967.

But they did pick up on the Z/28's nimble nature, which quickly proved itself more than worthy on SCCA tracks. Camaros dominated Trans-Am racing in 1968 and '69, action that thrust the Z/28 into the public limelight big-time. In 1968, sales of this hot-handling ponycar increased nearly ten-fold to more than 7,000, and the legend continued rolling on from there.

Though briefly shelved for two years in the Seventies, the Z/28 Camaro continued running strong into the new millennium before GM recently cancelled its F-body platform. Apparently all good things must indeed come to an end.

A huge 800-cfm Holley four-barrel fed the Z/28's 302 small-block.

Twin racing stripes on the hood and rear decklid were included in the Z/28 deal in 1967.

Chevrolet's Camaro joined Ford's ground-breaking Mustang in Detroit's ponycar corral in 1967.

Rally wheels and front disc brakes were standard on Chevrolet's first Z/28.

SPECIFICATIONS

Wheelbase: 108 inches

Weight: 3,070 pounds

Base Price: $3,380

Engine: 302 cubic-inch small-block V8

Compression: 11:1

Induction: single 800-cfm Holley four-barrel carburetor on aluminum high-rise intake

Horsepower: 290 at 5,800 rpm

Torque: 290 at 4,200 rpm

Transmission: Muncie four-speed manual

Suspension: independent A-arms w/coil springs in front; live axle with leaf springs and a radius rod in back, beefier springs and shocks at the corners

Brakes: power front discs, rear drums

Performance: 14.9 seconds at 97 mph in the quarter-mile, according to Car and Driver

Production: 602

1969 *Pontiac Trans Am*

General Motors recent cancellation of its fabled F-body platform, found beneath Chevrolet's Camaro and Pontiac's Firebird, also ended one of Detroit's lengthiest high-performance legacies.

Discounting Chevy's Corvette, which stands on its own as "America's sports car," Pontiac's Trans Am Firebird was the only musclecar to run uninterrupted from horsepower's heydays in the Sixties up into our new millennium. No, the Trans Am's cousin, Chevy's Z/28 Camaro, couldn't claim a similar streak: it was temporarily cancelled after 1974 then returned as a midyear model in 1977.

The Z/28 did come first, however, debuting in 1967. Pontiac's original Trans Am then followed two years later. Both cars were low-production, special-edition vehicles created with stock-class racing in mind—specifically the Sports Car Club of America's Trans American Sedan Championship series, originated in March 1966. In

Below: *Like so many American performance cars, Pontiac's original Trans Am experienced severe frontal lift at high speeds.*

order to legally compete a certain model on the SCCA circuit, a manufacturer had to sell a minimum number to the public. Additional SCCA specifications included a maximum displacement limit: 5 liters, or about 305 cubic inches.

Ford's Mustang, with its 289 cubic-inch small-block, fit comfortably into that category and dominated Trans-Am racing during its first two years. Chevrolet's Z/28 then sped past the Mustang to become the new SCCA champ in 1968 and 1969, and the "Trans-Am ponycar" race was on. By 1970 Dodge, Plymouth and even American Motors were selling hyped-up "homologation" hot rods intended to allow the parent company entry into the SCCA field.

Let's not forget Pontiac Motor Division, the firm that introduced the musclecar to America. In December 1968 the PMD boys introduced their Trans Am Firebird to the automotive press at

Riverside International Raceway in California, then followed that up with a public unveiling at the Chicago Auto Show in March 1969. Initially Pontiac's plan was to build enough T/A Firebirds to make them legal for SCCA competition, however long that roller coaster ride ran. Little did company officials at the time know that they were creating a long-running legend.

Curiously the car's Trans-Am racing career didn't take off as planned as a suitable SCCA-legal small-block V8 never reached regular production. The only engine offered for the 1969 Trans Am Firebird was a big-block V8 that displaced 400 cubic inches, 95 more than SCCA rules allowed. But, while the 400-powered Trans Am didn't qualify for the competition series it was named after it did delight the street-racing crowd and continued doing so better than the rest throughout the performance-starved Seventies and Eighties.

Listed under option code WS4 in 1969, the original "Trans Am Performance and Appearance" package was priced at about $1100 depending on transmission choice and bodystyle (coupe or convertible). Imagery was plentiful, what with that blue-accented Cameo White paint, fender-mounted air extractors, twin-scooped hood and rear spoiler.

Beauty beneath the '69 Trans Am's skin included a beefed up chassis consisting of a thickened one-inch front sway bar, heavier front coils and rear leaf springs, stiffer shocks, and a limited-slip Safe-T-Track differential. Brakes were power front discs, and quick, variable-ratio power steering was standard, too.

The base 400-cube engine was Pontiac's 335-horsepower "Ram Air III" rendition, coded L74. Another big-block, the 345-horse L67 Ram Air IV, was available at extra cost. A heavy-duty three-speed manual transmission was standard. Optional trans choices included wide- and close-ration Muncie four-speed manuals and GM's ever-present Turbo-Hydramatic auto-box. Only 55 of the 689 Trans Am coupes built for 1969 featured the hot L67. All eight '69 Trans Am convertibles were L74-equipped; four with automatic transmissions, four with manuals.

As a straight-line performer, the nose-heavy 1969 Trans Am was a real screamer, running in the low 14-second bracket for the

Above: *Trans Am buyers in 1969 could chose between four-speed manual and automatic transmission options.*

MILESTONE FACTS

- According to Pontiac engineer Herb Adams, the Trans Am's 60-inch-wide rear wing created 100 pounds of downward force at 100 mph.

- Pontiac's Trans Am was the only musclecar to run consecutively from the sizzling Sixties into the new millenium.

- With a big-block V8 beneath its hood, the nose-heavy 1969 Trans Am's weight bias was 58 percent up front, 42 percent in back.

- F70 fiberglass-belted rubber on 14x7 steel rims were standard for the 1969 Trans Am.

- Pontiac engineers originally planned to produce the Trans Am with a 303 cubic-inch small-block V8 to make it legal for SCCA racing. This engine did not make into production, leaving officials no choice but to install the 400-cube big-block, an optional Firebird power source since the 1967.

- Though engineers claimed the 1969 Trans Am's rear wing worked well creating downforce at speed, the car's nose did the opposite—unwanted front end lift was a real problem.

- Of the 697 Trans Am Firebirds built for 1969, eight were highly prized convertibles.

- Of the 634 L74-equipped Trans Am coupes built for 1969, 520 had four-speeds, 114 automatics. The model shown here features a four-speed

quarter-mile. And itt also did amazingly well in the twisties. Calling the new Trans Am "an animal; a souped-up, sharp-horned, hairy mountain goat, Sports Car Graphic magazine's road testers couldn't say enough about what was going on underneath. "We can't imagine where Pontiac learned how to set up a suspension, but this one is a good illustration that a nose-heavy car doesn't have to be a tragic understeerer." Added Hot Rod's Bob Swaim, " we feel safe in saying that, not counting Corvettes, the Trans Am is possibly the best handling production car made in this country."

True or not, this claim garnered little support on Mainstreet U.S.A. because so few first-edition Trans Ams were built in 1969. Production delays then almost left an even better T/A to a similar fate in 1970. But popularity soared from there, and Pontiac was selling more than 100,000 Trans Am Firebirds by 1979. In 1999, GM celebrated the Trans Am's 30th birthday with a special blue-accented white anniversary model.

A few years later the long, legendary tale came to a close.

SPECIFICATIONS

SWheelbase: 108.1 inches

Weight: 3,654 pounds

Base Price: $3,887

Engine: 400 cubic-inch Ram Air III V8

Horsepower: 335 at 5,000 rpm

Induction: single four-barrel carburetor

Transmission: four-speed manual

Suspension: independent A-arms w/coil springs in front; live axle with leaf springs in back

Brakes: power front discs, rear drums

Performance: 14.1 second at 100.78 mph in the quarter-mile (for Ram Air IV version)

Production: 689 coupes, eight convertibles

Pontiac engineers bragged about the downforce created by the Trans Am's rear wing (above). Sport wheels (right) were standard.

Production of L74/four-speed Trans Am coupes (shown here) in 1969 was 520.

PONTIAC

69 SUNSHINE STATE 70
10 - 8297
FLORIDA

1969 *COPO/Yenko Camaros*

When Chevrolet rolled out its big-block Super Sport Chevelle in 1965, GM edicts limited all its mid-sized A-body models to engines no larger than 400 cubic inches. The same lid applied to the new F-body Camaro when it was introduced in 1967.

Full-sized buyers could order the Corvette's 427 V8 all they wanted for their Impalas and Bel Airs, but Chevelle and Camaro customers had to "make do" with the 396, at least officially.

More than one quick-thinking dealer picked up where the factory left off and began swapping Corvette engines into Camaros in 1967. Most notable were the 427-powered ponycars that rolled off the lot at Yenko Chevrolet in Canonsburg, Pennsylvania. An experienced Chevy racer, Don Yenko had first tried modifying Corvairs for his speed-sensitive customers in 1965. He then turned his attentions to the new Camaro two years later.

The process began with a typical small-block F-body. Once at Yenko's shop, the tame 350 was yanked out and an L-72 427 was dropped in, along with lots of additional heavy-duty hardware and a little touch of extra eye-catching imagery. Presto, instant "Camaro Super Car," a complete package sold directly to the public. Sold as well were various options, including such things as traction bars, headers, rear gears as low as 4.88:1, a Vette-style fiberglass hood, sidepipes, spoilers and aluminum mags. Ultra-exotic L-88 equipment was also advertised for Yenko's SC Camaro.

Yenko's men made these time-consuming engine swaps for two years, using the SS 396 Camaro as a base the second time around in 1968. Then in 1969 they discovered Vince Piggins' central office production order (COPO) loophole, a somewhat clandestine paper trail normally used for special orders by fleet buyers, that is trucking firms, emergency groups, police departments, etc. COPOs didn't require upper office approval, so they represented an easy way to circumvent GM's dreaded displacement limits.

As Chevrolet's performance products chief, Piggins cleverly used the COPO pipeline to create various 427-powered F- and A-bodies right on Chevrolet assembly lines in 1969. COPO code number 9561 delivered a '69 Camaro armed with the iron-block L-72 427. The same application in the Chevelle lineup was coded COPO 9562. A third code, COPO 9560, belonged to the outrageous ZL-1 Camaro with its all-aluminum 427.

Reportedly, Don Yenko first met with Chevrolet officials in the summer of 1968 to discuss the use of COPOs to help simplify the

Yenko SC conversions. Although some believe that factory-built 427 Camaros might have been funneled from Chevrolet to Yenko in 1968, the accepted opinion holds that all 1967-68 Yenko Camaros were dealership swaps. All 1969 Yenko Camaros clearly were COPO cars.

A limited run of COPO 9561 Camaros were delivered to Canonsburg, where they were treated to a special dose of "Yenko/SC" (or "sYc" for short) imagery that made them all but impossible to miss on the street in 1969. "Yenko/SC" striping ran down the bodysides, and similar stripes (with "sYc" for short) went onto the hood. That same sYc nomenclature also was stenciled onto the bucket seat headrests inside. Back on the outside, "Yenko"

MILESTONE FACTS

- Don Yenko won four SCCA national titles driving Corvettes before he started marketing his own personal breed of Bow-Tie performance in 1965. First came his red-hot Corvair "Stingers," race-ready compacts that proved unbeatable at any speed.

- One of the 200 '65 Stingers built by Yenko Sportscars—the performance division of Yenko Chevrolet—scored its own SCCA national crown in 1966 with Jerry Thompson driving.

- The Daytona Yellow paint on the Yenko Camaro shown here was a special-order item.

- Yenko Chevrolet also began offering 427-powered Chevelles and Novas in 1969. Novas fitted with the Corvette's 350-cube LT-1 small-block V8 were introduced in 1970.

- Atlas aluminum wheels were Yenko Camaro options in 1969.

- Along with the L-72 427 V8, the COPO 9561 package also included 4.10:1 Positraction gears, a Muncie close-ratio four-speed, F41 sport suspension, and power front disc brakes.

- Another COPO option, coded 9737, added a beefier one-inch front sway bar, a 140-mph speedometer, and 15-inch rubber on Chevrolet's popular 7-inch wide Rally wheels. COPO 9737 was known as the "Sports Car Conversion."

- Yenko Camaro production was 54 in 1967, 64 in 1968

- Yenko Chevrolet also marketed modified Vegas in 1971

Above: *Pennsylvanian Don Yenko was one of various Chevrolet dealers to market hopped-up versions of the popular Camaro back in the Sixties.*

badges appeared on the fenders and rear cove panel, and "427" emblems were slapped onto the hood and tail.

As to how many COPO Camaros made up that limited run, that is not clear. Before his death in March 1987, Yenko claimed he ordered 500 COPO 9561 Camaros in 1969. Apparently supporting his claim is a widely circulated photo showing a sign proudly announcing Yenko's "350th 1969 unit built." Yet only 201 '69 Yenko Camaros have been documented. Some say the "350th unit" photo may have referred to all Yenko products (Camaros, Chevelles and Novas combined) for 1969.

All arguments aside, Yenko's Corvette-powered Camaro truly was a Super Car in 1969. Yenko rated the SC Camaro's 427 at 450 horsepower, more than enough muscle to make low 13s in the quarter-mile an easy reality.

Yenko continued toying with special performance conversions in 1970, in this case using only Novas. The Yenko Chevelle was a one-hit wonder for 1969, and the Yenko Camaro was dropped at year's end. As it was, GM's displacement limit disappeared after 1969, making regular production of the awesome LS-6 SS 454 Chevelle possible. With Chevrolet offering so much performance right out of the catalog in 1970, how could hot-blooded dealers like Don Yenko compete?

Though the Yenko Camaro was only around for three years it left an impression that still has teeth to this day.

The stencil on a Yenko Camaro's bucket seat headrest was short for "Yenko Super Car."

Chevrolet rated its L72 427 V8 at 425 horsepower. Yenko upgraded it to 450 horses.

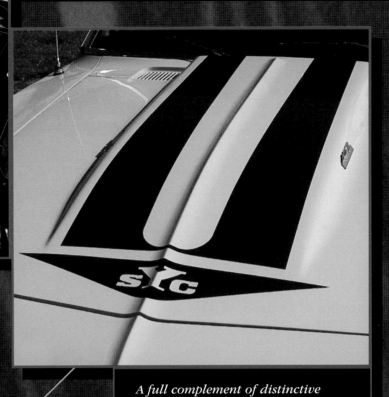

SPECIFICATIONS

Specs: 1969 Yenko Camaro

Wheelbase: 108 inches

Weight: 3,050 pounds

Engine: 427 cubic-inch L-72 Corvette V8

Horsepower: 450 at 5,000 rpm (rated by Yenko Chevrolet)

Induction: single 800-cfm Holley four-barrel carburetor

Transmission: Muncie M21 close-ratio four-speed manual

Suspension: independent A-arms w/coil springs in front; live axle with leaf springs in back

Brakes: power front discs, rear drums

Production: 201 are known

A full complement of distinctive striping and badges played a prominent part in Yenko's Super Car conversion in 1969.

THE
Heartbeat
OF AMERICA
YESTERDAY'S CHEVROLET

Five-spoke Atlas mags were optional for the '69 Yenko Camaro.

1969-70 *Ford Boss* 302 *Mustang*

In February 1968 Henry Ford II hired former General Motors executive Semon "Bunkie" Knudsen to run the show in Dearborn. Knudsen, the son of William Knudsen, the man who had left Ford for General Motors back in 1921, had become GM's youngest general when he'd started out at Pontiac in 1956.

Almost overnight, he then transformed your grandpa's car company into a builder of true excitement. "You can sell a young man's car to an old man," went his prime motto, "but you'll never sell an old man's car to a young man." In Bunkie's mind, young men liked hot cars, and the hotter the better.

"When Mr. Knudsen came from GM, he brought along a strong belief in the power of performance," explained Motor Trend's Eric Dahlquist. Knudsen also brought along a strong belief or two concerning the Mustang. In his words, the popular ponycar was "a good-looking automobile, but there are a tremendous number of people out there who want good-looking automobiles with performance. If a car looks like it's going fast and doesn't go fast, people get turned off."

Knudsen took one look at Ford's ponycar and decided it was time for a change. The Mustang had just been redesigned for 1967 with an eye towards making more room up front for more engine, but initial results were disappointing. Though the Cobra Jet Mustang did debut in April 1968, Bunkie wanted more, he wanted a hot machine that was as fast in the curves as it was in a straight line. That summer he demanded that his engineers produce "absolutely the best-handling street car available on the American market."

Something like Chevrolet's Z/28 Camaro perhaps?

Knudsen wasn't above stealing things—concepts or people—from his former employer. More than one GM genius also jumped over to Ford at Bunkie's invitation, and they brought more than one GM idea along with them. One of the more notable defectors was designer Larry Shinoda, the

man who had created the Z/28's sporty image in 1967. When Knudsen hired Shinoda in May 1968, his first assignment was to best that hot, little Camaro.

Shinoda's contributions included the new Mustang's stripes, spoilers and window slats, as well as its name. "I suggested they call it 'Boss,'" a groovy label his superiors initially had a tough time relating to. But once they were tuned in as to how hip it was to be "boss," they began diggin' it, man.

Ford contracted Kar Kraft Engineering, in Brighton, Michigan, to develop the Boss Mustang, and the first prototypes were completed by August 1968. Ford Engineering that took over production work from there. Engineer Matt Donner was the man responsible for the excellent Boss 302 chassis, which quickly impressed critics with the way it hugged the road. "Without a doubt the Boss 302 is the best-handling Ford ever to come out of Dearborn and may just be the new standard by which everything from Detroit must be judged," claimed a Car and Driver report.

How did the Boss 302 stack up to Chevy's hot-handling Z/28? "In showroom trim, car for car, the Mustang was close, but I can't really say [it] was superior," said Shinoda. On the track, the battle between the two arch-rivals was a toss-up. Chevrolet's Trans-Am Camaro took home SCCA racing laurels in 1969, while Ford's Boss 302 put the Mustang back on top in 1970.

As for street performance, both rivals relied on special 290-horsepower 302 cubic-inch small-block V8s. Base for Ford's Boss 302 was a modified Windsor block featuring four-bolt main bearings. On top of that went new cylinder heads then being readied for the upcming 351 Cleveland V8. With their big ports and large, canted-angle valves, these heads were excellent breathers.

Ford's Boss 302 Mustang was the Trans-Am racing champ in 1970, with Parnelli Jones' number 15 car taking top individual honors. At top is teammate George Follmer's Boss during pre-season testing.

MILESTONE FACTS

- Along with the Boss 302's high-profile image, designer Larry Shinoda was also known for his work on Chevrolet's stunning Corvette Sting Ray, introduced in 1963.

- Shinoda also named the car, but not without an argument. "They were going to call it 'SR-2,' which stood for 'Sports Racing" or 'Sports Racing—Group II,' which I thought was a dumb name," he recalled in 1981. "I suggested they call it 'Boss.'" His idea won out.

- Both the Boss 302 and Boss 429 Mustangs were developed by Ford contractor Kar Kraft Engineering in Brighton, Michigan.

- According to Ford engineer Bill Barr, the Boss 302 dyno tested at 314 horsepower with all equipment in place and working. In bare-bones form with no air cleaner and headers in place of the stock exhausts, the Boss 302 produced more than 390 horsepower.

- Boss 302 production in 1969 was 1,628.

- Race-car quick 16:1 manual steering was standard, as were big 11.3-inch front disc brakes. Ten-inch drums handled braking chores in back. Power assist for both brakes and steering was optional.

- Boss 302 updates for 1970 included expanded color choices; from the four offered in 1969—Bright Yellow, Acapulco Blue, Calypso Coral, Wimbledon White—to 13, including the truly radioactive trio of "Grabber" colors: Grabber Blue, Grabber Green and Grabber Orange.

- Appropriate "Boss 302" decals apparently were in the works for a third rendition in 1971 before the the Boss 302 V8 was dropped.

The Boss 302 suspension package developed by Donner involved, in his words, "mostly adjustments." Star of the show were super fat F60 Wide-Oval tires on wide 15x7 Magnum 500 wheels. To make room for all that extra tread, the Boss 302's front wheel arches were re-rolled to increase clearance. Remaining tweaks included typically stiffened springs and shocks, the latter coming from Gabriel.

In 1970, the second-edition Boss 302 Mustang received a sway bar at the rear end, and that was about it as far as mechanical advancements underneath were concerned. On top came a slightly revised image and more color choices. Easily the hottest new image item was Ford's optional Shaker hood scoop, which as functional at it was "boss-looking," it rammed cooler outside air into the carburetor whenever pedal met metal.

And that happened a lot in a Boss 302 Mustang, one of Detroit's best all-around performers of the original musclecar era.

Designer Larry Shinoda added the blacked-out panel surround the Boss 302's gas cap (left), the rear spoiler and back window slats (right)

The Boss 302 V8 (left) was rated at 290 horsepower. The super-cool "shaker" hood scoop (below) was optional.

SPECIFICATIONS

Wheelbase: 108 inches

Weight: 3,260 pounds

Base Price: $3,500

Engine: 302-cid Boss V8 with canted-valve "Cleveland" heads

Compression: 10.5:1

Induction: single 780cfm Holley four-barrel on an aluminum high-rise intake with optional "Shaker" hood scoop

Horsepower: 290 at 5,800 rpm

Torque: 290 at 4,300 rpm

Transmission: four-speed manual only

Suspension: independent A-arms w/coil springs in front; live axle with leaf springs and staggered shocks in back, thick sway bars at both ends.

Brakes: power front discs, rear drums

Performance: 14.62 seconds at 97.5 mph in the quarter-mile

Production: 7,013

1969-70 *Mercury Cougar Eliminator*

Mercury division always has offered quite a bit more prestige than its corporate cousin Ford. Yet it still has continually encountered difficulties earning its due regardless of how much quality awaited its customers. Then again, isn't that the fate of most middle children? Lower-priced Fords always sell like hotcakes, and the top-dog Lincolns will forever garner all the attention from top-shelf shoppers.

Whether or not Mercury will finally find its fair share of the limelight soon remains to be seen. As intriguing as Mercury's new performance sedan, the Marauder, was in 2003, it still rolled right into the shadows, much like so many other muscular Mercury models before it.

Take for example the Cougar Eliminator of 1969-70. As cool as they came during the days of Purple Haze and groovy go-go boots, Mercury's hottest-ever ponycar offered it all: pizzazz, performance

Below: *A prototype Eliminator debuted at the Los Angeles auto show.*

and prestige. Being a Cougar, the Eliminator was inherently more roomy and luxurious than its Mustang running mate, and even more class and convenience was available by way of a long, long options list.

Like the Boss 302 Mustang, the Cougar Eliminator was the work of the late Larry Shinoda, the design genius who had previously penned the '63 Sting Ray for Bill Mitchell at Chevrolet. When Bunkie Knudsen fled GM's executive offices for Ford's in 1968, he enticed Shinoda to make a similar defection, with the goal being to one-up Chevy's Z/28 Camaro with the Boss 302. Shinoda's bitchin' Boss image went over so well, Lincoln-Mercury officials then decided they should try the same tack.

Taking its name from the dragstrip, a prototype Cougar "Eliminator" was prepared for an October 1968 debut at the Los Angeles Auto Show. Spoilers front and rear fit the beautiful Cougar body like a glove and reportedly worked. Also part of the package was an aggressive hood scoop, bodyside striping, a blacked-out grille and wide Goodyear rubber on American Racing mags. Positive public response convinced L-M execs to rush this Boss Mustang knock-off to market as a mid-year 1969 model. Regular-production examples were introduced in March that year.

Save for the mags, the first Eliminator was essentially a carbon copy of the prototype. As much as Shinoda campaigned for a suitably sporty set of standard wheels for the '69 Eliminator, cost-conscious execs wouldn't budge; conventional 14x6 stamped-steel rims with mundane dog-dish hubcaps were included as part of the base package. At least attractive styled-steel wheels were offered at extra cost.

Standard equipment did include F70-14 Goodyear Polyglas tires and the Competition Handling Suspension group, which included heavy-duty front and rear springs and shocks and a large front anti-sway bar. A rear sway bar was optional. And like the flaming orange prototype, all regular-production Eliminators turned heads with ease thanks to six available eye-popping "Competition" paint choices.

Unlike its Mustang counterpart, which relied solely on the Boss 302 small-block, the '69 Cougar Eliminator was offered with various power sources. Base was the 351 four-barrel V8, the latest concoction of Ford's Windsor small-block family. A 320-horse 390 cubic-inch big-block was next up the ladder, with the 335-horsepower 428 Cobra Jet big-block topping things off. Ordering the Cobra Jet added an even stronger suspension with higher rate

MILESTONE FACTS

- In 1970, Ford Motor Company's hot, new 351 Cleveland V8 became the Eliminator's standard powerplant.

- As in 1969, the 428 Cobra Jet big-block V8 was an Eliminator option in 1970.

- Total Cougar Eliminator production (all engines) in 1970 was 2,200. Eliminator production in 1969 (again with all engines) was 2,411.

- Mercury's Competition Handling Package was standard beneath a 1970 Eliminator. Included was a thicker 15/16-inch front sway bar and a half-inch rear bar.

- Boss 302 Eliminators were sold only with four-speed manual transmission in 1970.

springs, a thicker front anti-sway bar and staggered rear shocks. The Eliminator's big hood scoop could've also been made functional atop a Ram-Air 428 CJ.

The bone-jarring Cobra Jet suspension was also included in a fourth Eliminator package, this one using the high-winding Boss 302 small-block with its superior canted-valve heads. Like its Boss Mustang brethren, the Boss 302 Eliminator represented a wonderful combination of straight-line strength and hot handling that made it one of the musclecar era's best all-around performers. While Cobra Jet Cougars were among Detroit's fastest machines of the day—forays into the 13-second bracket for the quarter-mile were no problem—they were no match for their small-block cousins on the long and winding road. The nose-heavy big-block Eliminator handled nowhere near as nicely as the better-balanced Boss 302 variety.

Yet as attractive as the Boss 302 Eliminator was in both 1969 and '70, it still fell well short of its Mustang cohort as far as popularity was concerned. The 1970 Boss Cougar shown here is one of only 450 built that year.

Clearly both the Eliminator and its Mustang counterpart had a lot to offer in 1970: great looks, lots of muscle and ample road-worthiness. But apparently there was only room in Ford Motor Company's ponycar corral for one Boss. And it was again left to a Mercury musclecar to lose its way in the shadows.

Shinoda's favored rear-deck spoiler (above) was a popular option for 1969 and 1970. The Eliminator name (right) also appeared in those years only.

Above: Distinctive sport wheels with trim rings were Eliminator options in 1970.

A four-speed stick (far left) was included behind the optional Boss 302 V8 (left).

Noted designer Larry Shinoda supplied the image for both Ford's Boss 302 Mustang and its Cougar Eliminator cousin. Distinctive striping and a blacked-out grille (above) were part of the Eliminator package in 1969 and 1970 (shown here), as was a chin spoiler.

SPECIFICATIONS

Wheelbase: 111 inches

Weight: 3,610 pounds

Base Price: $3,200

Engine: 302-cid Boss V8 with canted-valve "Cleveland" heads

Compression: 10.5:1

Induction: single 780cfm Holley four-barrel on an aluminum high-rise intake

Horsepower: 290 at 5,800 rpm

Torque: 290 at 4,300 rpm

Transmission: four-speed manual

Suspension: independent A-arms w/coil springs in front; live axle with leaf springs in back, sway bars front and rear

Brakes: front discs, rear drums

Performance: 14.4 seconds at 98 mph in the quarter-mile, according to Cars magazine

Production (with Boss 302 V8): 450

1969-70 Boss 429 Mustang

When Ford married its big, bad Boss 429 V8 to the Mustang in 1969, it did so to legalize the so-called "Shotgun" motor for NASCAR racing. According to NASCAR rules, any model or engine could compete as long as at least 500 regular-production examples were made available for public sale.

Those rules didn't specify that the two be built together, leaving Ford a loophole to roll right through. As long as the Blue-Oval boys brought 500 or more Boss 429 V8s to the dance, it didn't matter how they were dressed. On the street, the big Boss satisfied homologation standards beneath ponycar hoods. On NASCAR tracks, it then threw its weight around behind the extended snout of Ford's odd-looking Talladega, which, by the way, came standard in regular-production trim with a 428 Cobra Jet V8. Confused? You should be. Some things never change; NASCAR rules moguls still have heads spinning to this day.

Like the Boss 302, the Boss 429 Mustang was originally developed by Ford's performance contractor, Kar Kraft Engineering, in Brighton, Michigan. Kar Kraft then handled final production duties, rolling out its first Boss 429 in January 1969, nearly three months ahead of Ford's first Boss 302.

Development of the Boss 429 V8 dated back to 1968 after Ford had introduced its 385-series big-block family for its luxury lines. To take this mill racing, engineers recast a special reinforced cylinder block, then topped it off cast-iron heads featuring hemispherical combustion chambers. In production, those iron heads were traded for weight-saving aluminum units with revised combustion chambers that weren't quite hemispherical. Thus another nickname: "Semi-Hemi."

Whatever the name, the big Boss 429 did not drop easily into the ponycar platform, thus the reasoning behind Kar Kraft's involvement. Various labor-intensive modifications were required, including widening the engine compartment by two inches, and these

changes were best made on a small, specialized assembly line.

Ford started delivering '69 Mach 1s to the Kar Kraft works in December 1968. There the cars were stripped of their engines, and specially reinforced shock towers were engineered to supply the extra underhood room needed to allow the Boss 429 V8's entry. Upper A-arm location points in turn were moved outward an inch and lowered another inch. Beefier spindles were also installed, as was a modified export brace on top to firmly tie the restructured shock towers to the cowl.

On the outside went "flared" front fenders, needed to supply extra clearance for the standard F60 Wide-Oval rubber mounted on 15x7 Magnum 500 wheels. Other exterior mods

Right: *Complementing the Boss 302 Mustang was its big, bad brother, the Boss 429.*

MILESTONE FACTS

- According to Car Life magazine's critics, the Boss 429 Mustang was "the best enthusiast car Ford has ever produced."

- Unlike the Boss 302's super-clean shell, the Boss 429 body retained the 1969 SportsRoof Mustang's rear roof pillar medallions and fake rear quarter scoops.

- No striping or black-out treatment was added to the Boss 429, just simple, straightforward "Boss 429" decals for the front fenders.

- Standard Boss 429 equipment included power front disc brakes, power steering, staggered Gabriel shocks in back, and thick sway bars at both ends.

- Included with the Boss 429 V8 was a Drag Pack-style oil cooler to help keep lubricants within their effective temperature range.

- Also standard was a close-ratio four-speed that delivered torque to a Traction-Lok differential with 3.91:1 gears out back.

- Clearance was tight beneath a Boss 429 Mustang's hood. A thinned-down power brake booster was used to avoid a conflict on the driver's side with the Shotgun motor's huge valve cover. And the battery was relocated to the trunk, where it also conveniently transferred weight from the front wheels to the rears.

- Production of 1970 Boss 429 Mustangs was 499.

- Changes to the 1970 Boss 429 Mustang were few. Most noticeable was low-gloss black finish for that huge hood scoop. Mechanical upgrades included the addition of a standard Hurst shifter and the relocation of the rear sway bar from below the axle to above.

There was no mistaking the Boss 429 V8 with its "semi-hemi" heads.

were minor in comparison. The most prominent add-on was a huge functional hood scoop.

Beneath that scoop went three different variations of the Shotgun motor. The first 279 cars built were fitted with "S-code" engines. These NASCAR-style Boss big-blocks featured beefy connecting rods with large 1/2-inch bolts. The remaining Boss 429s for 1969 and most for 1970 got the "T-code" engine, which traded those heavy, rev-limiting rods for lighter pieces with 3/8-inch bolts. The first T engines featured the same hydraulic cam and magnesium valve covers found inside and on top of the S rendition. But early in the T run, the magnesium covers were replaced with aluminum units and a slightly more aggressive solid-lifter cam superseded the hydraulic stick. The third Boss 429 rendition, found in very few 1970 models, was the "A-code" engine, which was basically a T motor with revised smog controls. All three versions were conservatively rated at 375 horsepower.

As mean as the Boss 429 looked on paper, real-world results didn't quite measure up, at least in some opinions. More than one magazine road tester called the NASCAR-engined ponycar "a stone." In designer Larry Shinoda's words, the Semi-Hemi "was kind of a slug in the Mustang." On the other hand, Car Life's critics claimed that the big-block Boss "ranks as one of the more impressive performance cars we've tested."

Why the difference of opinions? Most in the know knew that the Boss 429 Mustang should have been running well into the 13s. Hell, Ford's Semi-Hemi was a full-fledged race engine unleashed on the street. But therein lay the problem. Engineers were forced to defeat their own purposes to make this monster streetable. The Boss 429's big valves and ports were designed to make lots of power at high rpm. Yet the cam, although aggressive by most perspectives, was not up to the task of fully filling those ports with fuel/air. On top of all that, the factory-installed rev-limiter turned off the juice just when the big Boss was just starting to show off its true potential.

As was the case with the Boss 302, the Boss 429 was built for two years only. Kar Kraft shipped off its final Shotgun-motored Mustang on January 6, 1970. Later that year Ford pulled the plug on its racing activities, and that was that. Such was life in the fast lane.

Far left: Big, sticky F60 Goodyear tires on 15-inch Magnum 500 five-spoke rims were standard for the Boss 429 in 1969 (shown here) and 1970.

Left: A competition-conscious oil cooler, mounted just ahead of the radiator core support on the driver's side, was also standard.

Ford people laughingly rated the Boss 429 big-block V8 at 375 horsepower.

This functional hood scoop was painted to match the Boss 429's body in 1969. It became black in 1970.

SPECIFICATIONS

Wheelbase: 108 inches

Weight: 3,870 pounds

Base Price: $4,868

Engine: 429 cubic-inch V8 with aluminum cylinder heads

Compression: 10.5:1

Induction: single 735-cfm Holley four-barrel carburetor on a dual-plane aluminum intake

Horsepower: 375 at 5,200 rpm

Torque: 450 at 3,400 rpm

Transmission: four-speed manual only

Suspension: independent A-arms (suspension geometry modified to make room for big Boss 429 V8) w/coil springs in front; live axle with leaf springs and staggered shock absorbers in back

Brakes: power front discs, rear drums

Performance: 14.09 seconds at 102.85 mph for the quarter-mile, according to Car Life test

Production: 857

BOSS 429

The Boss 429 V8 was basically a race engine let loose on the street.

1970 *American Motors* AMX

During the Sixties you could count the number of American-built two-seaters using only a couple digits, one finger for Chevrolet's Corvette, the other for American Motors Corporation's almost forgotten AMX. While the Corvette just celebrated 50 years on the road in 2003, the hot, little AMX lasted a mere three years, 1968 to '70, although AMC's diminutive machine probably deserved a much more noteworthy fate.

What was an AMX? Wags still commonly refer to it as little more than a cut-down Javelin, itself a sporty new AMC offering for 1968. At 97 inches, its truncated wheelbase was one click shorter than the Corvette's, and designers had achieved this short stance by simply wacking out 12 inches (in the area in front of the rear wheels) from the same unit-body platform found beneath the Javelin. With no room left for a backseat, the AMX simply featured a carpeted storage area in the shortened rear compartment. From there the two siblings from Kenosha, Wisconsin, shared fenders, doors, bumpers, rear deck lid, windshield and rear glass. Though optional V8 power was available for the Javelin (a six-cylinder was standard), the AMX came with nothing else.

Argument also still persist to this day as to which actually came first, although it must be said that the Javelin was introduced in the fall of 1967, with the AMX debut following nearly six months later. But the AMX was conceived first, its roots running back to January 1966 when the original AMX (for American Motors Experimental) concept-car appeared at the Society of Automotive Engineers annual gathering. This fiberglass-bodied flight of fancy featured seating for two and a short 98-inch wheelbase, and it also inspired the evolution of a steel-bodied, regular-production spin-off. A few evolutions later, the real-world AMX was unveiled to rave reviews on February 15, 1968, during Daytona Beach's famed Speed Weeks spectacular. Along the way designers also morphed the new platform into the longer, roomier Javelin. In truth, referring to the Javelin as a stretched AMX is probably the correct thing to do.

Styling wizard Richard Teague, who was responsible for the AMX's exceptional good looks, called American Motors' two-seater, "a hairy little brother to the Javelin." Group vice-president Vic Raviolo, himself directly responsible for once-staid AMC's startling walk on the wild side, referred to it as "a Walter Mitty Ferrari." And although the AMX—like the Camaro, Cougar and Firebird—essentially followed in the Mustang's hoofprints, its truly distinctive long-hood/really-short-deck profile nearly redefined the ponycar image. Toss in a decent dose of standard performance and the AMX almost qualified as a breed apart.

AMC officals foresaw great things ahead for their sawed-off runt, projecting sales of 10,000 for he abbreviated 1968 model year, and 20,000 for each year thereafter. Despite some positive early press, despite semi-stunning looks, despite impressive American-style performance, the AMX never took off as expected. A minor revamp for 1970 couldn't stave off fate, and sagging sales convinced the guys in Kenosha to make a short story even shorter. But blaming the quick disappearing act on the car itself isn't at all fair, especially when you consider the improvements made for 1970 to an already nice package.

Paying due homage to Teague's somewhat timeless sheetmetal lines, not a crease was touched or a bauble added to clutter things

MILESTONE FACTS

- Total two-seat AMX production for 1968 to '70 was 19,134: 6,725 in 1968, 8,293 in 1969 and 4,116 in 1970.
- According to Mechanix Illustrated's Tom McCahill, American Motors' two-seat AMX was "the hottest thing to ever come out of Wisconsin."
- Mechanically speaking, the '70 AMX was updated with a switch from AMC's old trunnion setup to ball-joints in the front suspension.
- After the two-seat AMX was retired after 1970, American Motors continued using the name for its top-shelf Javelin model—which did have a backseat.
- A Hurst shifter was standard equipment for four-speed AMX's in 1970.
- AMC also offered its coveted "Go Pac" options group for the '70 AMX. Included were power front disc brakes, a special handling package, a 3.54:1 Twin-Grip differential, E70 Goodyear red-line tires, and exterior "C-stripes."

up, with the possible exception of 1970's new hood, which was lengthened two inches and crowned with an aggressive "power bulge." Unlike the 1968-69 hood, which was fully non-functional, the '70 AMX bonnet could be put to work once the optional ram-air equipment was in place.

Beneath that new hood was new standard power as the previously installed 225-horse 290-cid "Typhoon" V8 was replaced by a 360 V8 rated at 290 horsepower. The top option continued to be AMC's big 390, but it was now rated at 325 horses, 10 more than in 1968 and '69.

Elsewhere, simulated "sidepipe" rocker trim was added and the parking lights were moved from the bumper to the grille, supposedly leaving the bumper openings to supply cooling air to the brakes. Anyone with eyes, however, could see the ducts installed for that purpose didn't extend close enough to the brakes to make any real difference.

But most who looked at the '70 AMX liked what they saw. And in 1985, the Milestone Car Society recognized American Motors' intriguing two-seater as an American milestone, citing its styling, engineering, performance and innovation. If only it had been born in Detroit instead of Kenosha—we might still be talking about the AMX today.

Left: *Craig Breedlove established 106 speed and endurance records at a Texas test track with two 1968 AMX coupes.*

A "rim-blo" steering wheel and simulated woodgrain appointments were new for the 1970 AMX.

Left: Functional ram-air equipment was included as part of AMC's "Go Package" options group.

AMC's two-seat AMX was built for 1968-70 only.

SPECIFICATIONS

Wheelbase: 97 inches

Weight: 3,495 pounds

Base Price: $3,560

Engine: 390 cubic-inch V8

Induction: single Carter four-barrel carburetor

Compression: 10:1

Horsepower: 325 at 5,000 rpm

Torque: 420 at 3,200 rpm

Transmission: four-speed manual

Suspension: independent A-arms w/coil springs in front; live axle with leaf springs in back

Brakes: power front discs, rear drums

Performance: 14.68 seconds at 92 mph in the quarter-mile, according to Motor Trend

Production: 4,116

AMC's 325-horse-power 360 cubic-inch V8 became the AMX's standard engine in 1970.

1970 *Dodge* Challenger R/T

Short for "Road and Track," "R/T" was to Dodge what "SS" was to Chevrolet, though in comparatively smaller doses. Dodge built nowhere near as many R/T models as Chevrolet shelled out Super Sports during the Sixties and Seventies, nor did the former cars pack as much of a high-profile whallop as the latter.

Those "R/T" badges were cool, and they did signify the presence of a special machine. But they never attained the status of, say, "SS 396" or "SS 454."

From its humble beginnings in 1967, the R/T package included, first and foremost, a high-powered big-block Magnum V8. Chassis beefs were thrown as part of the deal, too, to better handle the R/T's extra muscle. First came the Coronet R/T that year, followed by a Charger R/T in 1968, both of which were fitted with either the "standard" 375-horse 440 cubic-inch V8 or the optional 426 Hemi. A third R/T, this one based on Dodge's all-new ponycar platform, debuted for 1970.

Plymouth's ponycar, the Barracuda, had been around since 1964, and in 1967 it had graduated up into Chrysler's A-body ranks, home to Dodge's Dart. Along with this slight upsizing came the opportunity to stuff big-block V8s beneath the Barracuda's long hood, although that optional addition left little room for anything else under there. Say, like a compressor for optional air conditioning.

Below: *Striping was standard for the Challenger R/T in 1970. The vinyl roof and rear spoiler were options.*

Merry Mopar men then set out to rebuild their ponycar platform with an eye towards creating more space up front for both more engine and more equipment. Though overall size remained compact as ever, the all-new E-body foundation they came up with relied on a cowl structure borrowed from Chrysler's mid-sized B-body line (Coronet, Road Runner, etc.), which meant for a wider, roomier engine bay compared to the A-body Barracuda's. From there followed a truly spunky little car conveying a rakish image accentuated by its abbreviated tail perched high above the road out back.

Dodge designers, led by Bill Brownlie, managed to create a slightly different slant on the same long-hood/short-deck theme by using slightly more wheelbase, 110 inches compared to 108 for Plymouth's remade 1970 Barracuda. They then named their E-body "Challenger," and they offered it in three forms: the basic six-cylinder model, the more sporty V8, and the aforementioned R/T. All three model lines in turn featured three different bodystyles: a hardtop, a convertible, and a "sports hardtop" featuring Dodge's Special Edition package, which among other things included a vinyl-covered roof with a downsized rear window.

Contrary to its midsized predecessors, the Challenger R/T was powered in base form by Dodge's 383 cubic-inch Magnum four-barrel V8, rated at 335 horsepower. Next up the extra-cost pecking order was the 375-horse 440, followed by the 390-hp triple-carb 440 and the ever-present Hemi. Both of the 440 big-blocks and the 425-horse 426 were offered as options for the R/T only.

A three-speed manual was the standard gearbox behind the 383 Magnum, but Chrysler's always-tough three-speed Torqueflite automatic was optional, as was a preferred four-speed. Buyers opting for the Hemi or one of the 440s got a choice between the four-speed or the Torqueflite.

Additional standard Challenger R/T features in 1970 included Dodge's Rallye suspension, heavy-duty drum brakes, and Wide-Tread F70x14 tires (Hemi models rolled on larger 15-inch wheels and tires). The Rallye instrument cluster was part of the deal inside, and the R/T's outside could be dressed up with either a longitudinal

MILESTONE FACTS

- Dodge built 76,935 Challengers in various forms (coupes and convertibles, six-cylinder and V8 power, etc.) in 1970.

- Total Challenger R/T hardtop production (import and domestic) in 1970 was 14,889. Of that figure 2,802 were fitted with the 440 V8—1,886 with automatic transmission, 916 with four-speeds.

- Another 3,979 R/T hardtops with the upscale Special Edition package were also built for 1970, as were 963 R/T convertibles.

- The Special Edition package included a vinyl-covered roof with a small rear window, though the vinyl top (with normal-sized glass) could be ordered individually for the basic Challenger R/T hardtop.

- Standard on a 1970 Challenger R/T was the Rally instrument cluster, which included a simulated woodgrain panel, a 150-mph speedometer, a tachometer, a trip odometer, clock, and gauges for fuel, oil and temperature. An ammeter and three-speed variable wipers were also part of the package.

- Dodge unveiled an interesting new pallet of exterior shades for the 1970 Challenger, including such eye-catching colors as "Plum Crazy" (shown here), "Sublime," and "Go-Mango."

stripe or Dodge's popular "bumble-bee" stripe around the tail.

Among popular options were Dodge's familiar Rallye road wheels and the too-cool "Shaker" hood scoop, added midway through the 1970 model run. The Shaker was both functional and fun; when it was doing its dance you knew that things below were really cookin', and all that heat was helped along by the cooler, denser ambient atmosphere sucked in through that vibrating scoop. The Challenger R/T's basic twin-scooped hood looked downright dull in comparison.

Dodge picked out a handful of professional race drivers to promote its 1970 model line, and drag racing's "Big Daddy" Don Garlits was assigned the Challenger R/T. As Garlits was quoted in company ads, "Now Dodge has gone and done the real thing. They watched the whole ponycar thing develop, then built their own super-tough version. Compact like a Dart. Wide like a Charger. Just the right size for anyone who likes his own personalized backyard bomb. Dodge should sell a million of 'em."

While production fell a bit short of that prediction, the Challenger R/T nonetheless didn't disappoint—whether you were a Dodge dealer or a customer in search of the hottest thing out there wearing a Pentastar in 1970.

Dodge's 375-horsepower 440 Magnum V8 (above) was one of three engines offered for the Challenger R/T. The popular Rallye wheels (upper right) were optional.

A sporty interior (left) and competition-style fuel filler (below) was standard fare on all 1970 Challengers.

SPECIFICATIONS

Wheelbase: 110 inches

Weight: 3,820 pounds

Base Price: $3,266 (with "standard" 383 V8)

Engine: 440 cubic-inch Magnum V8

Induction: single Carter four-barrel carburetor

Compression: 9.7:1

Horsepower: 375 at 4,600 rpm

Torque: 480 at 3,200 rpm

Transmission: four-speed manual

Suspension: independent A-arms w/torsion bars in front; live axle with leaf springs in back

Brakes: four-wheel drums, standard; power front discs, optional

Performance: 14.8 seconds at 95 mph in the quarter-mile, according to Sports Car Graphic

Production (w/440 V8 and four-speed): 916

Dodge first offered its "R/T" performance package in 1967.

1971 *Plymouth Hemi'Cuda*

Chrysler Corporation initially didn't have a specific model able to compete directly with all those GTOs and SS 396s flooding from General Motors factories during the mid-Sixties. But Mopar men did have an engine more than capable of putting the muscle in musclecar—the fabled 426 Hemi.

Built in sparse numbers from 1966 to '71, the Hemi was rated the same each year: 425 horsepower. Actual output, however, was more like 500 horses, a plain fact that seat-of-the-pants responses supported with ease. Even when bolted into those rather mundane Dodge Coronets and Plymouth Satellites in 1966 and '67, the mean, nasty Hemi could still produce quarter-mile times in the high 13s—exciting performance indeed.

Various cooler mid-sized B-body Mopars were fitted with the rare Hemi option during its short, happy run from 1966 to '71, including Dodge's Charger and Super Bee and Plymouth's GTX and

Road Runner. But in most minds, the best Hemi of 'em all came in a slightly smaller package. And that package debuted just before the musclecar class reached the end of its own short road.

New for 1970 in both Dodge and Plymouth ranks were two E-body ponycars. Dodge's was the fully fresh Challenger, while Plymouth's carried a familiar name: Barracuda. Introduced in 1964, Plymouth's first flying fish inspired an enthusiastic following even though it wasn't much more than a yeoman Valiant with fastback glass tacked on in back. It was treated to a revamped A-body platform and a new look all its own in 1967, and new that year as well was optional big-block power. Plymouth designers then introduced the hip "'Cuda" image in 1969.

Even groovier was the redesigned E-body Plymouth, which first appeared on drawing boards in Cliff Voss's Advanced Styling Studio in 1967. Voss's main goal was make more room up front for more engine. Squeezing a big-block between A-body flanks had not been easy, and extra underhood space for options like power steering, power brakes and air conditioning had been all but impossible to come by. Not so in the E-body's case.

Even the Hemi fit comfortably beneath an E-body hood in 1970. How did designers manage to seemingly stuff 10 pounds of stuff into a five-pound bag? By basing the E-body foundation on the bigger B-body's cowl structure, thus creating a much wider engine bay for Plymouth's new Barracuda. Spunky, rakish sheetmetal, credited mostly to stylist John Herlitz, wrapped things up on top to give the third-generation predator-fish a truly distinctive appearance.

Accentuating sporty impressions even further was the latest 'Cuda rendition, which came

Above: *What's shakin', baby? In 1970 and '71, it was Plymouth's groovy "Shaker" hood scoop, which attracted stares wherever it went.*

standard with the 335-horse 383 big-block V8 and was dressed up with front foglamps, hood pins, simulated hood scoops, a blacked-out rear panel, and "hockey stick" bodyside stripes that

Above: Hemi 'Cuda convertibles were as rare as they were fast— only seven of these 1971 models were built.

- Along with Plymouth's new E-body platform in 1970 came three distinct ponycar model lines, the base Barracuda with its standard budget-conscious six-cylinder, the sporty 'Cuda, and the prestigious Gran Coupe with its leather buckets and overhead console.

- All Hemi V8s built from 1966 to '71 were fed by two 650-cfm Carter four-barrel carbs on an aluminum manifold. All were also rated at 425 horsepower

- Hemi updates in 1968 included a hotter cam, revised valvetrain and a windage tray inserted inside the six-quart oil pan.

- Yet another revised cam (same lift, less radical "ramps") appeared in 1970 along with hydraulic lifters in place of the previously used solid tappets, improvements made with an eye towards "civilizing" this big ape.

- Plymouth built 652 Hemi ''Cuda coupes in 1970; 284 with four-speeds, 386 with automatics. Another 14 'Cuda convertibles were also ordered with Hemi power that year.

- Total Hemi 'Cuda production in 1971 was 114: 107 coupes and seven convertibles. Of those coupes, 59 had four-speeds, 48 had automatics. Five of the convertibles were automatic-equipped.

- Big, fat F60 treads on 15x7 Rallye wheels were mandated for the Hemi 'Cuda.

"mandated" when the Hemi engine option was chosen, and the new "Shaker" hood scoop was standard. Additional cast members included a 9-3/4-inch Dana rear end and a choice between a four-speed or the tough Torqueflite automatic.

Simply sticking right out through the hood, a Shaker scoop did just as its name implied whenever pedal met metal and a Hemi started rockin'. But looking cool wasn't its only function; it also allowed those twin Carter carbs below draw in cooler, denser outside air.

A heavy-duty radiator was of course also mandated for the Hemi 'Cuda, as were large 11-inch drum brakes all around and a beefed-up foundation. Ad called Hemi 'Cuda underpinnings "the ruggedest ponycar suspension in the industry." "The front suspension is the same extra-heavy-duty combination used on Hemi Road Runners and GTXs—the same torsion bars, shock absorbers, anti-sway bar, spindles, ball joints, etc," continued that ad copy. "Ditto the rear suspension, which carries two extra half-leaves in the right rear spring, to prevent torque steer off the line."

Once off that line, the '70 Hemi 'Cuda produced some of the most frightening quarter-mile times ever published during the musclecar era. After a little tinkering, Car Craft's crew managed a startling 13.10-second quarter-mile pass. No wonder many witnesses still call this Camaro-eating E-body the greatest of the Hemis—if not the greatest of all musclecars.

Plymouth built Hemi 'Cudas again for 1971 before the end finally came for unbridled horsepower. Nonetheless, Chrysler's littlest Hemi still loomed large in the memories of horsepower hounds for years to come, and still does today. Big time.

incorporated engine displacement identification at their tails. Three numbers could've been stuck on: 340, 383 or 440.

Those hockey sticks simply read "Hemi" when the optional 426 was specified. The 425-horse V8 was only available for the 'Cuda, which then took on the "Hemi 'Cuda" name even though it wasn't officially an individual model. All 'Cuda accoutrements were thus

This full loaded 1971 Hemi 'Cuda interior includes instrumentation, bucket seats and a console. Both four-speeds and automatics were installed behind the Hemi.

All 'Cuda models featured racing style hood pins.

Foglamps up front were standard too for Plymouth's 'Cuda line.

SPECIFICATIONS

Wheelbase: 108 inches

Weight: 3,800 pounds

Original price: $4,300, approximate

Engine: 426 cubic-inch Hemi V8

Compression: 10.25:1

Induction: two Carter four-barrel carburetors

Horsepower: 425 at 5,000 rpm

Torque: 490 at 4,000 rpm

Transmission: four-speed manual

Suspension: independent A-arms w/torsion bars in front; live axle with leaf springs in back

Brakes: heavy-duty four-wheel drums, standard (power front discs, optional)

Performance: 13.10 second in the quarter-mile, according to a Car Craft test of a 1970 model

Production (Hemi 'Cuda convertible w/four-speed): 2

Fender "gills" (below) were new additions for the 1971 Barracuda. The optional Shaker (right, 1970 edition shown) was available atop other engines besides the Hemi.

SHAKER

1971 *Ford Mustang* BOSS 351

Fans of Ford ponycar performance were hit hard when both the small-block (302) and big-block (429) Boss Mustangs were unceremoniously cancelled in 1970. But not all was lost. In November that year, Dearborn officials rolled out their new Boss 351, a truly hot 1971 Mustang based on the totally restyled SportsRoof body, as fast a fastback as yet come down the pike.

The heart of the '71 Boss 351 was the 351 High Output (HO) Cleveland V8, an able small-block that could throw its weight around like most big-blocks. Rated at 330 horsepower, the HO featured superb free-flowing heads, which were nearly identical to those used by the Boss 302 save for revised cooling passages. Those excellent canted valves carried over from Boss 302 to HO right down to their diameter, as did much of the valvetrain. Both engines also shared screw-in rocker studs, hardened pushrods, and guide plates. The Boss 351's solid-lifter cam, however, was more aggressive than the Boss 302's.

The 351 HO's lower end was also more stout. As was the case inside the Boss 302's modified Windsor block, the HO's crank was held in place by four-bolt mains, but the latter had four-bolt caps at all five main bearings, not just three. The HO crank was cast (of high nodular iron) instead of forged, and it was specially tested for hardness. Forged connecting rods were shot peened and magnafluxed and were clamped to the crank by super-strong

3/8-inch bolts. Pistons were forged-aluminum pop-up pieces. On top was a 750-cfm Autolite four-barrel on an aluminum dual-plane manifold.

The Boss 351's standard supporting cast included a ram-induction hood, a special cooling package with a flex fan, and a Hurst-shifted wide-ratio four-speed. In back was a Traction-Lok 9-inch rearend with 31-spline axles and 3.91:1 gears. Underneath was the Competition Suspension package, which featured heavier springs, staggered rear shocks, and sway bars front and rear. Power front disc brakes were standard, too, as were F60 raised-white-letter rubber tires on 15x7 steel wheels adorned with the flat hubcaps and trim rings. Ford's flashy Magnum 500 five-spoke wheels were optional.

Below and above rightight: *Able to smoke through the quarter-mile in the 13-second range, the Boss 351 Mustang ranked among Ford's hottest all-time musclecars.*

The Boss 351's standard appearance features were all but identical to those found on the 1971 Mach 1. Included up front was Ford's functional "NASA hood, a chin spoiler and a honeycomb grille with color-keyed surround. That ram-air hood incorporated twist locks and was done in either an argent or blacked-out finish, depending on the body paint choice. Like the hood, Boss 351's standard lower-body paint accents and accent tape stripes were either black or argent, again depending on the chosen exterior finish. Black or argent treatment once more showed up at the rear. And among remaining features were dual racing mirrors and "Boss 351 Mustang" decals on the fenders and tail. A rear deck spoiler was optional. The coveted Mach 1 sports interior was optional inside, while full instrumentation was standard.

Inside or out, from nose to tail, the Boss 351 Mustang was a big winner in most critics' minds. Sure, some reviewers complained about visibility problems inherent to the 1971 SportsRoof restyle. But they couldn't deny the Boss 351's aggressive appearance and high-spirited nature. Few rivals could keep pace. As Car and Driver reported, the Boss 351 "offers dragstrip performance [14.1 seconds at 100.6 mph] that most cars with 100 cubic inches more displacement will envy." Enthusiastic Motor Trend testers pushed the envelope even further, producing a 13.8-second run, a figure that put the Boss 351 right up there with the hottest Fords ever built.

Many witnesses at the time recognized too that the Boss 351 probably represented the end of the road for Ford's brand of muscle. "This is probably the last chance you'll have to buy a machine of this kind," began Sports Car Graphic's March 1971 Boss

351 road test. "Ford is now diverting all its racing talent and dollars into solving safety and pollution problems and trying to satisfy government mandates. We have heard from reliable sources that for the '72 new model release, all Ford products will be detuned to run on regular fuel. That means lower compression. The current exhaust-popping 11:1 [ratios] will probably be lowered 15 to 20 percent, and the only way to regain the lost power is through expensive modifications—which will probably become illegal. Perhaps we'll just learn to live with the situation, like war and taxes, which we accept as facts of life. But we have few years left. We might as well take what we can get and live it up while we can."

A few years? Who was kidding whom? Although the 351 HO did survive for one more year—albeit in detuned form—the Boss 351 Mustang came and went as quickly as it ran from stoplight to stoplight. One year here then gone.

At least the Boss Mustang legacy went out with a bang.

MILESTONE FACTS

- Ford's 351 Cleveland small-block V8 would carry on as the company's top performance powerplant after the 429 Cobra Jet big-block was cancelled in 1971.

- According to Lee Iacocca, Ford's Mustang had grown into "a fat pig" by 1971. But apparently bigger was better in the mind of Ford chief Semon "Bunkie" Knudsen, who had given the go-ahead for the "SportsRoof" restyle before he had been fired in 1969.

- Nearly everything about the 1971 SportsRoof was bigger compared to the 1970 fastback Mustang. It was three inches wider, two inches longer and 400 pounds heavier. Wheelbase was stretched an inch and both front and rear tracks increased two inches.

- Lee Iacocca took over for Knudsen atop Ford in 1970, and four years later he rode herd over a new breed of ponycar, the compact Mustang II, a car that he felt ran closer to its roots.

- The Boss 351 and Mach 1 Mustangs shared numerous appearance features, but the 351 HO small-block was exclusive to the Boss in 1971.

- Ford's use of the term "NASA hood" was actually a misnomer. The scoops on those hoods were actually known as "NACA" ducts around aviation circles. NACA, the National Advisory Committee for Aeronautics, was superseded by NASA, the National Aeronautics and Space Administration, in the late Fifties. Apparently Ford officials felt the American public in 1971 would recognize NASA, but not NACA.

The 330-horse 351 V8 (left) and a Hurst-shifted four-speed (far right) were standard; 15-inch Magnum 500 wheels (above) were optional.

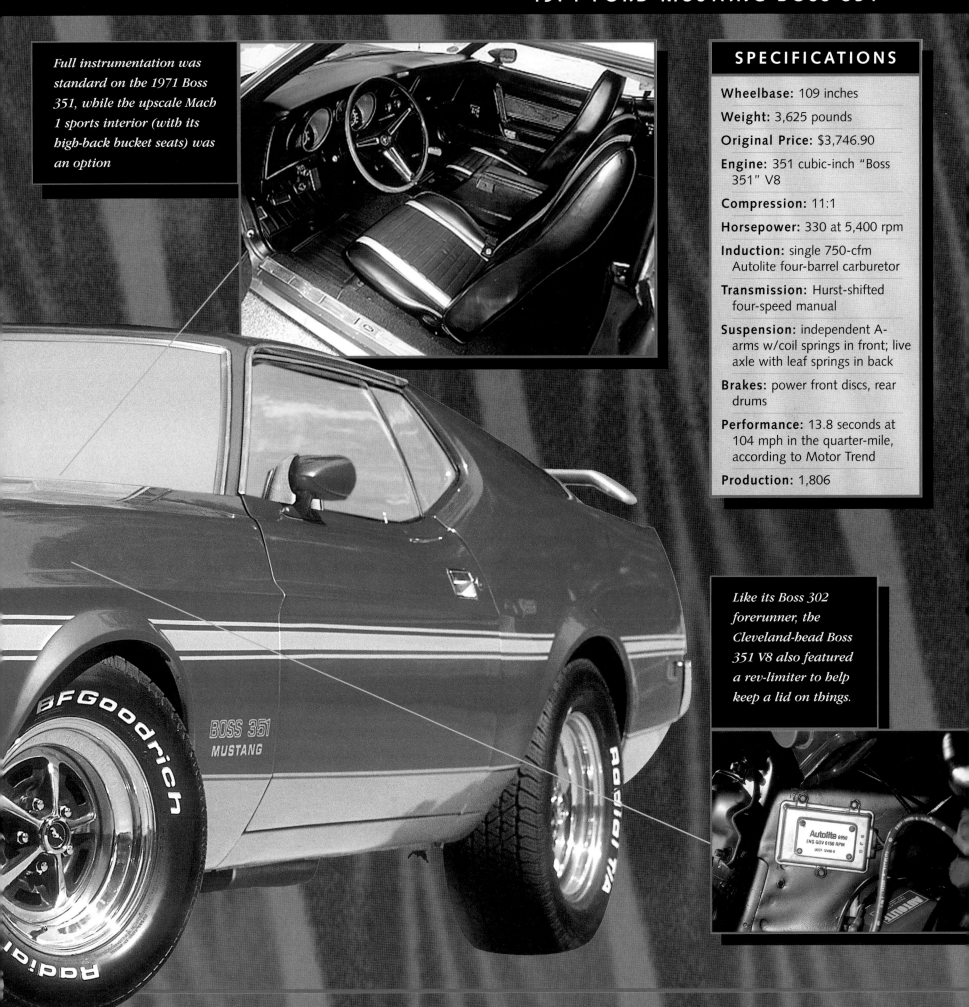

Full instrumentation was standard on the 1971 Boss 351, while the upscale Mach 1 sports interior (with its high-back bucket seats) was an option

SPECIFICATIONS

Wheelbase: 109 inches

Weight: 3,625 pounds

Original Price: $3,746.90

Engine: 351 cubic-inch "Boss 351" V8

Compression: 11:1

Horsepower: 330 at 5,400 rpm

Induction: single 750-cfm Autolite four-barrel carburetor

Transmission: Hurst-shifted four-speed manual

Suspension: independent A-arms w/coil springs in front; live axle with leaf springs in back

Brakes: power front discs, rear drums

Performance: 13.8 seconds at 104 mph in the quarter-mile, according to Motor Trend

Production: 1,806

Like its Boss 302 forerunner, the Cleveland-head Boss 351 V8 also featured a rev-limiter to help keep a lid on things.

BOSS 351
MUSTANG

1970 *Chevy Chevelle* LS-6 SS 454

Determining which car ruled during the musclecar era of the Sixties and Seventies is not an easy task—so many hot cars, so much hot-to-trot horsepower. Yet as tough as this task appears, it simply begs to be done. After all, competition was the musclecar's main claim to fame. The race had to have a winner, right?

Being the quickest from point A to B alone, however, did not a champion make. Granted, raw speed and power were top priorities. But not all performance-minded car buyers 30-something years back wanted to go racing. Most simply wanted to play the Walter Mitty part while driving to work, cruising the town, or picking up the younguns from John F. Kennedy Elementary.

If elapsed times are used as the only measuring sticks, Detroit's factory super-stocks of the early Sixties come out on top hands down. But these wild beasts were never meant for the street. In the civilized world they were nothing more than warranty work waiting to happen. Then again, so too were many of the mass-marketed musclecars to follow. Living with a fully pumped-up performance car in the Sixties was never easy, especially so when the package included solid lifters, lumpy cams, metallic brake linings, knee-

Below: *Free-breathing closed-chamber heads with big valves (2.19-inch intakes, 1.88 exhausts) and huge ports were key to the 450-horsepower LS6 454 V8's success.*

bending clutches, and locking differentials. More muscle almost always meant more headaches. No pain, no gain, right?

So where does this leave us as far as crowning our king?

Many believe that honor belongs to the Chevy clan. From a popularity perspective, Chevrolet's Super Sport Chevelle ranked as the musclecar era's front-runner. After finally succeeding the GTO as America's best-selling musclecar in 1969, the SS Chevelle outsold its rival from Pontiac by 37 percent before the axe came down on high-performance in 1972.

Chevrolet's SS 396 Chevelle rose to the top because it offered decent performance at a decent price in base form. "Although [the SS 396] is not the fastest machine right off the showroom floor, it does possess much more potential than any other car in its field," concluded Popular Hot Rodding's Lee Kelley in 1968. "The best-selling Supercar isn't the quickest," added a 1970 Car Life review. "But it looks tough. And it's kind to women and children. With the handling package, brakes, etc., the SS 396 makes a fine family car."

By 1970 the SS 396 legacy had grown so respected, Chevrolet's hype-masters didn't dare toy with it after the Turbo-Jet big-block had been bored out to 402 cubic inches late in 1969. "Ess-Ess-four-oh-two?" Nah. It was "Ess-Ess-three-ninety-six" or nothing at all—unless, of course, "it" was the new SS 454, the supreme evolvement of the breed.

The SS 454 Chevelle came into being after GM finally dropped its 400-cube maximum displacement limit for its intermediate models after 1969. Two widely different SS 454s were offered for 1970, beginning with the relatively tame LS5, rated at 360 horsepower. The other was the legendary LS6, a burly big-block that Car Life called "the best supercar engine ever released by General Motors." Many other critics considered the LS6 to be the best supercar engine, period.

Put together with care at Chevrolet's big-block V8 production plant in Tonawanda, New York, the LS6 was specially built from oil pan to air cleaner with super performance in mind. Unlike the LS5, which was based on a two-bolt main bearing block, the LS6's bottom end was held together with four-bolt main bearing caps. The LS6 crank was a tough forged steel piece cross-drilled to insure ample oil supply to the connecting rod bearings. Rods too were forged steel, and they were magnafluxed for rigidity.

The real attraction of the LS6 show was a pair of closed-chamber cylinder heads that could breathe with the best of them thanks to large rectangular ports and big valves. A huge 780-cfm Holley four-barrel fed this beast, which was conservatively rated at

MILESTONE FACTS

- The LS6's 450-horsepower factory rating was the highest ever assigned during the musclecar era of the Sixties and Seventies. Estimates put actual output as high as 500 horses.
- LS6 454 V8s were equipped with three different types of air cleaners in 1970: a conventional dual-snorkel unit, a jazzy chrome-topped open-element type, and the Cowl Induction design that sealed to the hood's underside to direct cooler outside air into the carburetor.
- Estimates put LS-6 convertible production for 1970 at between 20 and 70.
- Although magazines road-tested a 1971 LS-6 Chevelle, it never reached production. Instead, Chevrolet transferred the LS-6 option over to the Corvette lineup, where it too was offered for one year only.
- Chevrolet produced the SS 454 Chevelle from 1970 to 1972.
- Chevrolet later revived the LS-6 engine identification when it introduced the Z06 Corvette in 2001.

450 horsepower. Some claim actual output was more than 500 horses. Whatever the number, the results on the street were outrageous.

"Driving a 450-horsepowe Chevelle is like being the guy who's in charge of triggering atom bomb tests," claimed a Super Stock report. "You have the power, you know you have the power, and you know if you use the power, bad things may happen. Things like arrest, prosecution, loss of license, broken pieces, shredded tires, etc."

Even so, your mama probably could've driven this car down the quarter-mile in a click more than 13 seconds. Dipping into the 12s was only a matter of letting mom slap on a pair of slicks and bolt on a set of headers while her cookies cooled on the ledge. Either way, the LS6 Chevelle was all but unbeatable on the street. "That's LS as in Land Speed Record," concluded Motor Trend's A. B. Shuman.

But the LS6 SS 454 was not only a mean machine, it could also get along relatively well with everyday use. Evidence of just how well this wild animal could survive in domestication appeared in production figures. Even though the 450-horse 454 alone cost $1,000 extra, the slightly cranky LS Chevelle actually outsold its more affordable, less disagreeable LS5 brother, 4,475 to 4,298. Relatively speaking, Detroit's most powerful musclecar was also its greatest sales success.

Whether or not was the overall number one musclecar is your call.

Called "Cowl Induction," Chevy's ram-air system was optional on both the SS 396 and SS 454.

Above: Hood pins with tie-down cables were standard for the Super Sport Chevelle in 1970.

A standard speedometer (above) could barely hold the LS6, which was equipped with either a four-speed or automatic transmission (right).

SPECIFICATIONS

Wheelbase: 112 inches

Weight: 3,885 pounds

Original Price: $4,475

Engine: 454 cubic-inch LS-6 V8

Induction: single four-barrel carburetor

Compression: 11.25:1

Horsepower: 450 at 5,200 rpm

Torque: 500 ft-lbs at 3600 rpm

Induction: single 780-cfm Holley four-barrel carburetor

Transmission: Muncie "Rock Crusher" (M-22) four-speed manual

Suspension: independent A-arms w/coil springs in front; live axle with coil springs in back

Brakes: power front discs, rear drums

Performance: 13.12 seconds at 107 mph for the quarter-mile, according to *Car Craft* magazine

Production: 4,475 (coupes and a few convertibles)

1970 *Plymouth Superbird*

When a factory wants to go racing it must meet certain "homologation" standards. Various sanctioning bodies have had different standards over the years, but most have involved a minimum production requirement. In NASCAR's case back in the late-Sixties, the sanctioning body belonged to big Bill France.

And his homologation rule was simple: build 500 regular-production examples of any given engine or body style and you could race them all day long on his tracks.

That requirement, instituted in 1967, inspired Detroit to create some of the wildest street machines ever seen. Easily the wildest were Dodge's Charger Daytona and Plymouth's Superbird, built in 1969 and '70, respectively. Both looked like they were travelling 200 mph even while standing still. But unlike so many other fast-looking cars that were only imposters, these two high-flying machines did actually run that fast, in racing trim that is. Those bodies were fully function from an aerodynamic perspective, this because Detroit designers had finally discovered that brute force wasn't the only key to speed. Five-hundred or more horses could only do so much with a stock body, and apparently 175 mph was the limit. Breaking through that buyer required something more—something like a wind-cheating body.

Ford Motor Company racers breached that wall first when the sleek Fairlane and Cyclone fastbacks appeared in 1968. The Dodge boys then responded that fall with their slicked-up Charger 500. Taking its name from Bill France's production requirement, the aerodynamically refined '69 Charger 500 was put together at Creative Industries in Detroit. Using the grille from a '68 Coronet, the Creative fellows transformed the Charger's recessed frontal cavity into a flush nose, complete with fixed headlights. In back, they fabricated a steel plug to fill in the rear window tunnel. Presto! An additional 5 mph on top end.

While it initially looked promising from NASCAR perspectives, the Charger 500's early announcement, made before the 1968 season, only helped inspire quick retaliation from the competition. As Dodge

was showing off its new aero-racer in Charlotte, Ford was busy building a similar machine, the Fairlane-based Talladega, which featured a downward sloping nose that reduced frontal area and induced the air flow up over, not under. This helped the Talladega stay exceptionally stable while busting the 190-mph barrier on NASCAR superspeedways. Mercury also manufactured a kissin'-cousin to the Talladega in 1969, the Cyclone Spoiler Sports Special, or Cyclone Spoiler II.

Debuting in February 1969, the Talladega overwhelmed its counterparts from Dodge as LeeRoy Yarbrough's long-nose Fairlane won the Daytona 500. Talladega drivers claimed 26 races in 1969, Charger 500s 18, and Spoiler IIs four.

Then Dodge regrouped, returning in April 1969 with an even more aggressive aero-racer, the Charger Daytona, the product of some serious wind-tunnel

Right: *Aerodynamic improvements made at both ends of Plymouth's 1970 Superbird translated into 200-mph speeds on NASCAR superspeedways.*

testing. To better beat the breeze, Creative Industries added a pointed steel beak with a chin spoiler, a fully functional modification that stretched the car by about a foot and a half. In back went a cast-aluminum "towel rack" wing towering over the rear deck. And like the Charger 500, the Daytona was also fitted with a leaded-in steel plug to allow the installation of a flush rear window. Reportedly the new nose could produce nearly 200 pounds of downforce; that huge rear wing, 650 pounds. In full-race form, the Daytona was the first NASCAR competitor to surpass the 200-mph barrier.

Not long afterward, Plymouth designers kicked off their own aero-car project. Born in June 1969, then temporarily canceled in August, the Superbird was rapidly readied for the 1970 NASCAR season. As in the case of the Talladega-Spoiler II relationship, Plymouth's winged street racer looked similar to its Daytona forerunner from Dodge, but was very much of a different feather. For starters, the Road Runner front clip wouldn't accept that nose graft as easily as the Charger's did. Thus, a hood and front fenders were copped from the Coronet line for this application. Various measurements also differed at the nose and tail.

MILESTONE FACTS

- Differences between the Charger Daytona and Plymouth Superbird were many, but perhaps most noticeable was the Superbird's vinyl roof—added to hide the hand-leaded seams around the flush rear window's mounting plug.

- The metal noses on the Daytona and Superbird differed in various ways. The Superbird's nose cap sweeps upward slightly; the Daytona's snout doesn't. Air inlets were also located differently. The chin spoilers, however, were identical.

- Compared to the Daytona's spoiler, the Superbird's wing was taller and swept backward at a sharper angle. Its pedestal bases were also wider. Daytona wings used three-piece tape stripes done in three contrasting colors; red, white or black. Superbird wings were always body-colored.

- Though they're commonly referred to as "air extractors," the scoops on a Superbird's fenders were actually used in NASCAR configuration to allow extra clearance for the huge tires used in stock car racing. On the street, these rounded scoops were for looks only. The "flat-topped" scoops on the Daytona actually covered a meshed opening that allowed trapped air to exit from the front wheel wells.

- Three different engines were offered for the 1970 Superbird: the 375-hp 440 with single four-barrel, the 390-hp 440 Six Barrel, and 425-hp 426 Hemi.

- Total Superbird production in 1970 was 1,935: 1,084 with the 440 four-barrel, an additional 716 with the 440 Six Barrel V8, and 135 with the vaunted 426 Hemi.

Production figures too differed greatly as NASCAR homologation standards changed for the 1970 season. The minimum production requirement was now either 1,000 or a number equal to half of that company's dealers, whichever was higher. Plymouth officials were then faced with the task of creating nearly four times as many Superbirds as Dodge did Daytonas.

Once on the track, the two winged Mopars took command in 1970. Superbirds won eight races, Daytonas four. Another victory was scored by a Charger 500. The tally at Ford was four wins each for the Talladega and Cyclone Spoiler II, these recorded before Henry Ford II finally decided to cancel his corporation's competition programs late that year.

Bill France did the rest, instituting a carburetor restrictor plate rule for the high-flying Hemi-powered Mopars to help keep speeds (and the cars themselves) down to earth. This restriction then helped convince Chrysler officials to give up on the Superbird. Like the Daytona, it was a one-hit wonder.

A "towel-rack" rear spoiler (near left) adorned with Road Runner graphics (far left) was an unmistakable standard feature on the 1970 Superbird. Plymouth's popular Rally wheels (right) only complemented the high-flying image further.

1970 PLYMOUTH SUPERBIRD

Left: The 425-horsepower 426 Hemi was optional for the 1970 Superbird. Plymouth's 440 was standard.

Below: Air extractor scoops on Superbird fenders were non-functional.

SPECIFICATIONS

Wheelbase: 116 inches

Weight: 3,840 pounds

Base Price: $4,298

Engine: 426 cubic-inch Hemi V8

Compression: 10.25:1

Horsepower: 425 at 5,000 rpm

Torque: 490 at 4,000 rpm

Induction: two Carter four-barrel carburetors

Transmission: three-speed Torqueflite automatic

Suspension: independent A-arms w/torsion bars in front; live axle with leaf springs in back

Brakes: front discs, rear drums

Performance: 14.26 seconds at 103.7 mph for the quarter-mile, according to Road & Track (440 cubic-inch V8 model tested)

Production (with Hemi V8): 135; 77 with automatic transmission, 58 with four-speed manual

1970-71 *Ford Torino Cobra*

After paying dearly for the rights to Carroll Shelby's "Cobra" image, Ford officials wasted little time sticking Shelby's revered snake label on almost everything that moved. Make that everything that really moved.

First came the famed 428 Cobra Jet V8 in 1968. That was then followed in 1969 by a CJ-powered mid-sized muscle machine intended to follow in the Plymouth Road Runner's tracks. This new beast's name? What else?

With low-buck investment being the goal, the '69 Cobra was based on the yeoman Fairlane (in both formal-roof and fastback forms), not the top-dog Torino as is often commonly mistaken. Forget what you saw on NASCAR tracks; David Pearson's 1969 Grand National champion Talladega may have screamed "Torino" in on its quarter-panels, but there was nothing Torino about its street-going, long-nose counterparts. And the same was true for the non-aerodynamic Fairlane Cobra.

This confusion, however, was cleared up in 1970 when Ford's Better Idea guys did what they probably should have done in the first place, that is elevate the Cobra into the upscale Torino ranks. But this time only one bodystyle was offered, the newly restyled and renamed "SportsRoof," a sleek, sloping shape that had simply been called a fastback in previous years. As for the name game, the second-edition Cobra was unmistakably a Torino, it said so right there on the hood.

Below: Introduced as a Fairlane model in 1969, Ford's mid-sized Cobra became a top-shelf Torino offering the following year. A blacked-out hood with tie-down pins was standard.

Beneath that hood, perhaps as a trade-off for the Cobra's newfound top-shelf surroundings, was a little less standard venom. In place of the formidable 428 Cobra Jet was the 360-horse 429 Thunder Jet, a torquey 385-series big-block best suited for turning pulleys on air conditioning compressors and power steering pumps for the LTD/Thunderbird crowd. Called "Ford's new clean machine" by Motor Trend, the 385 big-block family was a product of Washington's increasingly more demanding mandates to reduce emissions. "Racing and research not only improve the breed," wrote MT's Dennis Shattuck, "they also clear the air."

While the typical 429 was kind to the environment, it did have an alter-ego, a dark side that better suited the jet set. To keep up with a box-stock '69 Fairlane Cobra, a '70 Torino Cobra customer had to shell out an extra $164 for the 429 Cobra Jet, a 370-horse variation on the 385-series big-block theme. Dearborn engineers took the relatively tame 429 Thunder Jet and added a 715-cfm Rochester Quadra-Jet four-barrel on a cast-iron, dual-plane intake. They also bolted on a pair of Cobra Jet cylinder heads, they with their large rounded intake ports and big valves—2.242-inch intakes, 1.722-inch exhausts. Compression was upped to a whopping 11.3:1, and a long-duration cam was stuffed inside.

The 429 Cobra Jet also could've been ordered with or without ram-air equipment. Even though that distinctive "Shaker" hood scoop surely helped whip up a few more ponies on the top end, engineers chose not to adjust the ram-air 429 CJ's advertised output, which mattered very little anyway considering that 370 horsepower was undoubtedly an understatement to begin with.

Equally understated was the output figure assigned to the 429 Super Cobra Jet, a truly beefy big-block that came along as part of the Drag Pack group. The Drag Pack option transformed a 429 CJ into an SCJ by adding a big 780-cfm Holley four-barrel and a long-duration, solid-lifter cam. Additional heavy-duty hardware included forged pistons, four-bolt mains and an external oil cooler. Completing the Drag Pack cast was either a 3.91:1 Traction-Lok or 4.30:1 Detroit Locker rearend. Like the "basic" CJ, the underrated 375-horsepower Super Cobra Jet could've been crowned with the Shaker scoop, which again failed to change the advertised output figure. After Super Stock's hot-foots managed a sensational 13.63-second quarter-mile blast in a '70 SCJ Cobra, it became more than clear that quite a few more horses were hiding in there somewhere.

MILESTONE FACTS

- Ford's 385-series big-block engine family was first offered in 1968 in both 429- and 460-cube forms.

- Motor Trend named the new Torino SportsRoof model its "Car of the Year" for 1970.

- The 429 Super Cobra Jet Torino Cobra ranked right up with the strongest musclecars ever built during the Sixties and early-Seventies.

- The SportsRoof body was 1.2 inches lower and 5.1 inches longer than the mid-sized fastback shell seen in 1969.

- Both the Magnum 500 wheels and "Shaker" hood scoop appearing on this '70 Torino Cobra were options.

- Ford introduced its Cobra as a Fairlane model in 1969. In 1970, it was elevated to topline Torino status and the optional 429 Cobra Jet replaced the standard 428 CJ used the previous year.

- A Hurst-shifted four-speed manual transmission was standard for the Torino Cobra in 1970. High-back bucket seats and a center console were optional.

- Torino Cobra production was 7,675 in 1970, 3,054 in 1971.

- Engine breakdown for 1970 Torino Cobra productionw as 3,213 base 429 Thunder Jet V8s, 974 429 Cobra Jets without optional Ram-Air equipment, and 3,488 429 CJ big-blocks with Ram-Air.

All CJ Cobras in 1970, Super or otherwise, were fitted with the Competition Suspension package, which typically added higher rate springs. Included as well was a stiff 0.95-inch front stabilizer bar and heavy-duty Gabriel shocks. On four-speed cars, the Gabriels in back were staggered, with one mounted in front of the axle, the other behind. This was a popular Ford trick used to hopefully control rear wheel hop created by axle wind-up during hard acceleration.

Like its Super Cobra Jet big brother, the CJ Cobra was no slouch when it came to putting those staggered rear shocks to the test in 1970. A February 1970 Motor Trend road test produced equally sensational performance figures for the 370-horse/four-speed Cobra. Zero to 60 mph required only 5.8 seconds, while the quarter-mile went by in 13.99 ticks at 101 mph—numbers no one dared sneeze at.

Ford offered the Torino Cobra again in 1971 before giving up on high-performance to concentrate on cleaner-running, more efficient cars. It would be more than 10 years before Blue Oval muscle again made the Detroit scene.

SPECIFICATIONS

Wheelbase: 117 inches

Weight: 4,185 pounds

Base Price: $3,249 (429 Cobra Jet option added $229 to this amount)

Engine: 429 cubic-inch Cobra Jet V8

Horsepower: 370 at 5,400 rpm

Induction: single 715-cfm Rochester Quadra-Jet four-barrel with "Shaker" hood scoop

Transmission: four-speed manual with Hurst shifter

Suspension: independent A-arms w/coil springs in front; live axle with leaf springs in back

Brakes: front discs, rear drums

Performance: 0-60 mph in 5.8 seconds, 13.99 seconds at 101 mph for the quarter-mile.

Production: 7,675

The Cobra's optional tachometer (above) may have been a failure (it was tiny and poorly located), but there was no knocking the standard Hurst shifter (left).

Ford paid Carroll Shelby for the rights to his "Cobra" image (above). Bright Magnum 500 wheels (left) were optional for the 1970 Torino Cobra.

Though not as dramatic as Chrysler Corporation's "Shaker," Ford's similarly designed optional ram-air hood scoop nonetheless fit the Cobra image to a "T."

1971 Plymouth GTX 440+6

Plymouth people waited three years before finally following Pontiac's lead. That is, wrapping up one of their hotter big-block V8s with a too-cool-for-school image to match. In 1964, anyone who was anyone recognized a GTO when they saw one.

While the same couldn't exactly be said in 1967 when Plymouth's GTX debuted, at least Chrysler's low-priced division had its face in Detroit's high-performance image race, and that was better than nothin'.

Not that Plymouth at the time didn't have enough more than muscle to offer the hot-to-trot crowd. Introduced for 1966, the 426 Hemi was as mean a mill as they came in those days. But Plymouth didn't do the Hemi any favors when it planted it between the flanks of Satellites and Belvederes, cars that didn't announce their presence in quite the same sexy way, say, as an SS 396 Chevelle did.

To help turn more heads, Plymouth designers took their trimmed-out, top-shelf Belvedere hardtop and altered its ego into the GTX street-prowler. Up front was a new hood featuring two scoops, both non-functional. On the left rear fender was a competition-type fuel filler, and bright exhaust tips ended the standard dual exhaust system in back. Twin racing stripes were optional for the hood and rear deck, while bucket seats were included in the deal inside. Groovy red-line Goodyear tires were standard at the corners, as was a heavy-duty suspension underneath.

Beneath those two dummy scoops was a standard V8 that then stood tall as the industry's largest displacement engine, the 440.

Introduced the previous year for Chrysler's luxury liners, this RB-series big-block was created by boring out the 426 wedge-head V8. In 1967, better-breathing heads, a warmer cam, and a free-flowing intake crowned by a single four-barrel carb transformed this lukewarm mammoth into Plymouth's Super Commando 440, a 375-horse monster that put the action behind the GTX's new image.

"It's exciting to look at and it's exciting to drive," wrote Hot Rod's Dick Scritchfield in honor of the 440-powered '67 GTX. "It's a model that has taken Plymouth out of the domestic snapshot album and put it right in the middle of the performance picture, and with a very sharp image I might add."

Only one optional engine was offered for the GTX, and its name was spelled H-E-M-I. But either way, with the base 440 or extra-cost 426, the '67 GTX was a real winner.

In 1968 the GTX was joined by its less-expensive Road Runner running mate, itself powered by a standard 383 Commando. Like the GTX, the Road Runner too could've been fitted with the optional Hemi, but then that kinda defeated its budget-conscious purpose, didn't it?

A new power choice appeared for both Plymouths in 1970, the 440 "Six Barrel." This triple-carb big-block had first appeared the year before as part of a no-nonsense, race-ready package based on both the Road Runner and Dodge's Super Bee. The engine option alone was then extended to GTX (and Coronet R/T) buyers in 1970.

In Plymouth terms, the 440 Six Barrel V8 replaced the 440 Super Commando's single Carter four-barrel with three Holley two-barrels on an Edelbrock aluminum intake. Internal additions included

Left: *Radioactive paint, glaring graphics and an optional rear-deck spoiler made this 1971 GTX a real head-turner, even while standing still.*

MILESTONE FACTS

- Total GTX production for 1971, foreign and domestic, was 2,942.

- Plymouth's Satellite was the base model for the 1971 GTX; earlier GTXs were based on the Belvedere, which was retired after 1970.

- Chrysler's triple-carb 440 V8 debuted in 1969 as part of a special performance package based on mid-sized B-body models. Both Dodge's "440 Six Pack" Super Bee and Plymouth's "440 Six Barrel" Road Runner were stripped-down, race-ready rockets that put the "bare" in bare bones. Neither came with wheelcovers or even hood hinges—their lightweight fiberglass lids simply lifted off by hand after four pins were released at the corners.

- Plymouth's 440+6 V8 was a $125 option for the 1971 GTX. It cost $262 beneath a '71 Road Runner's hood.

- The 426 Hemi was a $750 option for the '71 GTX. Only 30 were built.

stiffer hemi valve springs, beefed-up rocker arms and connecting rods, and flash-chromed valves. Output was advertised at 390 horses.

GTX customers could again chose between Plymouth's three big-blocks—the standard 440 four-barrel, the triple-carb 440 and the 426 Hemi—in 1971, but this time around they got to wrap all that Mopar muscle up in all-new sheetmetal. A truly fresh restyle for Plymouth's mid-size lineup produced softer lines and subtle contours, just what you'd expect from a Seventies musclecar. A wide choice of wilder than wild colors also added to the attraction, as did optional spoilers and that zany "Air Grabber" hood with that crazy toothy grin painted onto the sides of the vacuum-operated flap that opened up at speed to let cooler, denser air into the carb below.

Or carbs. For 1971, the 390-horse 440 was officially named the "440+6" V8, a tidy $125 option for the GTX. As in previous years, Plymouth's triple-carb big-block was offered with either the Torqueflite automatic or four-speed manual—no wimpy three-speeds here. Both choices were good, it all depended on how much you liked gear-jamming.

Plymouth customers who liked the 440+6 GTX didn't have much of a choice by the end of 1971. The musclecar's days were all but through, and Chrysler's legendary Hemi and triple-carb 440 were both cancelled that year. Same for the subtly cool GTX, a big-block brute that may not have wowed the musclecar crowd like the GTO and others, yet still inspired a faithful following.

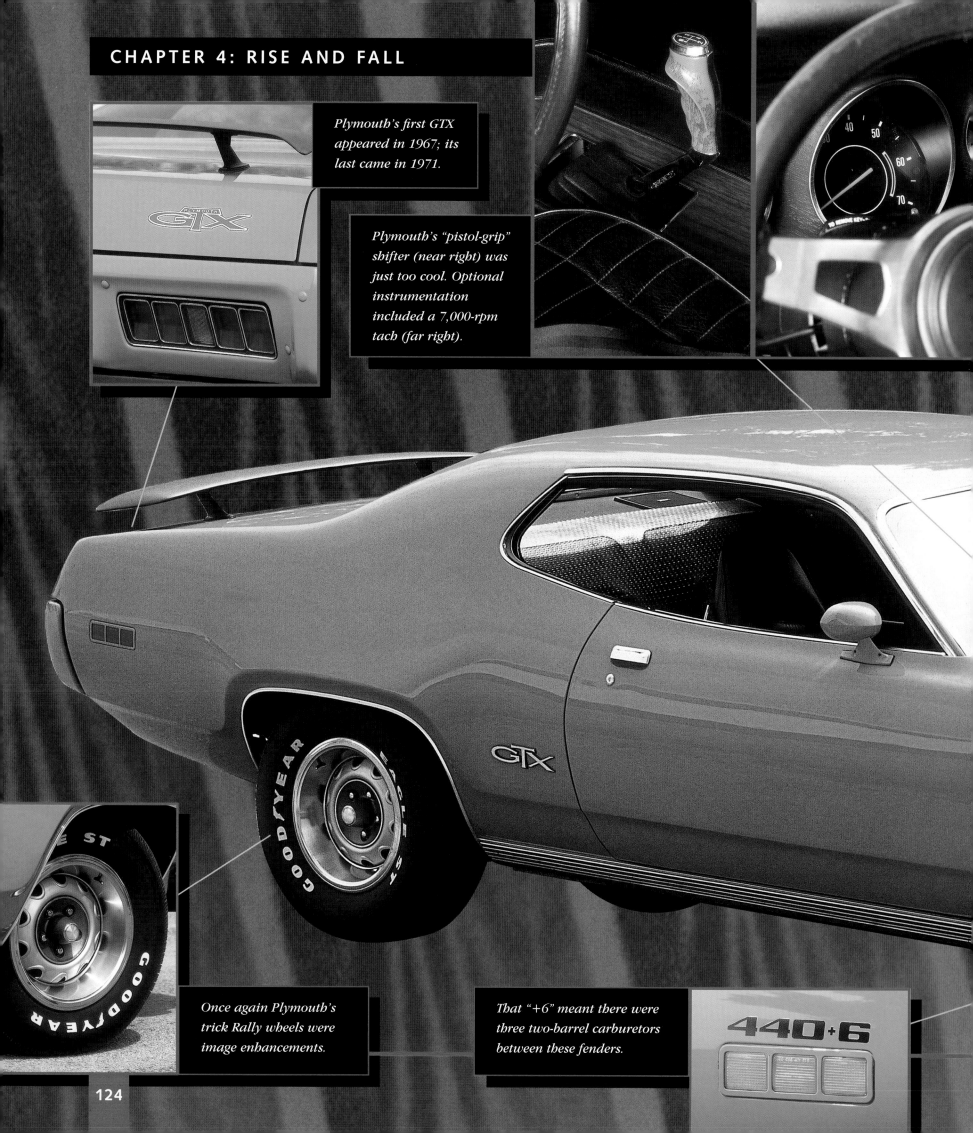

Plymouth's first GTX appeared in 1967; its last came in 1971.

Plymouth's "pistol-grip" shifter (near right) was just too cool. Optional instrumentation included a 7,000-rpm tach (far right).

Once again Plymouth's trick Rally wheels were image enhancements.

That "+6" meant there were three two-barrel carburetors between these fenders.

Plymouth's entertaining "Air Grabber" hood (left) was a GTX option, as was the 390-horsepower 440+6 big-block V8 (below).

SPECIFICATIONS

Wheelbase: 115 inches

Weight: 4,022 pounds

Base Price (for standard GTX w/440 four-barrel): $3,707

Engine: 440 cubic-inch V8

Induction: three Holley two-barrel carburetors

Compression: 10.5:1

Horsepower: 390 at 4,700 rpm

Torque: 490 at 3,200 rpm

Transmission: four-speed manual

Suspension: independent A-arms w/torsion bars in front; live axle with leaf springs in back

Brakes: four-wheel drums, standard; power front discs, optional

Performance: 15.02 seconds at 96 mph for the quarter-mile, according to Motor Trend test of a similar 440+6 1971 Road Runner

Production: 135; 73 with automatic transmission, 62 with four-speed

125

1973-74 *Pontiac Trans Am* 455 Super Duty

Detroit's original musclecar era came and went every bit as quickly as the mean machines themselves traveled from stoplight to stoplight. Pontiac's GTO officially kicked things off in 1964, and within 10 years it was all over save for the shouting.

But wouldn't you know it? It was Pontiac that again marked a high-performance milestone by giving us the last "great American musclecar." While rival engineers in Detroit were busy trading mph for mpg, Pontiac people continued building excitement in 1973 and '74, and they called this four-wheeled fun the 455 Super Duty Trans Am.

Arab oil embargoes and federal emissions standards notwithstanding, Pontiac engineers still somehow managed to unleash what may well have represented the company's best musclecar to date—and that, of course, was saying a lot. At the heart of this amazingly emissions-legal beast was the LS2 455 V8, a thoroughly modern big-block that, even with its hydraulic cam and relatively mild compression, still could've easily blown away most of Detroit's unfettered, atmosphere-choking supercar V8s had it debuted five years earlier. Was it any wonder then that PMD officials felt this engine was worthy of a name that had made performance history a decade earlier? "Just when we had fast cars relegated to the museum section, Pontiac has surprised everyone and opened a whole new exhibit," claimed a 1973 Car and Driver report on the 455 Super Duty.

Everything about the 455 SD V8 was super-duper, from its new beefy block, to its burly nodular-iron crank, to its bullet-proof forged-iron rods. A heavy-duty oil pump, 8.4:1 TRW forged-aluminum pistons, a Rochester Quadra-Jet four-barrel, and free-flowing cast-iron headers were also included. But the key to the whole works were the heads, which were tweaked within an inch of their lives by the horsepower-making gurus at Air Flow Research to flow better than anything Pontiac engineers had ever concocted. The end result was a low-compression big-block that made 310 real, net-rated horses while still remaining kind to the environment. Or was it?

Clever PMD engineers noticed that EPA engine testing only ran for about 50 seconds. They then accordingly developed a system that shut off the required exhaust gas recirculation valve after 53

seconds, allowing the 455 Super Duty to breathe easier—and breathe out unacceptable emissions concentrations—after initially passing emission testing with supposed flying colors. Clean-air cops, however, smelled a rat. The ruse was quickly discovered, and Pontiac people were forced to remove their EGR inactivating system and retest the Super Duty by March 15, 1973. A less-aggressive cam was required to pass these tests. Advertised output then dropped to 290 horsepower. Even so, the 455 Super Duty remained a formidable force.

The 455 SD was originally introduced, in 310-horse form, to the press by Special Products Group chief Herb Adams on June 28, 1972, at GM's Milford Proving Grounds. Adams promised the Super Duty option would be available by that fall for the Grand Am, Grand Prix, LeMans and both Firebirds, Trans Am and Formula. Those testing hassles, however, delayed initial deliveries of the "detuned" 290-

Above: *Pontiac devotees were familiar with the Super Duty (SD) moniker, which first appeared during the early Sixties for a collection of factory race cars.*

horse 455 SD until April 1973, and only then for the two Firebirds.

The 455 Super Duty F-body shocked the automotive press, most of whom were already convinced they'd already witnessed the

MILESTONE FACTS

- Most witnesses agree that Pontiac created the musclecar in 1964; many also support the claim that the 455 Super Duty Trans Am was the last great musclecar.

- Pontiac's famous "Super Duty" moniker had been used first to identify the race-ready 389 and 421 V8s that debuted in 1961 and '62, respectively.

- The 455 Super Duty V8 went into 300 Firebirds in 1973: 252 Trans Ams and 48 Formulas. Another 1,000 were built the next year: 943 Trans Ams and 57 Formulas.

- The Trans Am's corporate cousin, Chevrolet's Z28 Camaro, was temporarily discontinued after 1974. But Pontiac's "screaming chicken" kept running right on through these troubled times and remained arguably America's only surviving musclecar until the Z/28 returned in 1977.

- Standard wheel size was 15x7. Two styles were offered in this size, the familiar Rally II or the polycast Honeycomb.

- Transmission breakdown for 1974 Super Duty Trans Am production was 731 automatics, 212 manuals.

- Transmission breakdown for 1973 Super Duty Trans Am production was 180 automatics, 72 manuals

- Styling updates in 1974 traded the '73 Firebird's round headlights for rectangular units.

- Reportedly the LS2 455 V8 could rev safely to 6,000 rpm and run strongly on 91-octane fuel.

- Total Firebird production in 1974 was 73,729

- Total Trans Am production in 1974 was 10,255.

musclecar's last stand. "The Last of the Fast Cars comes standard with the sort of acceleration that hasn't been seen in years," announced Car and Driver in a May 1973 road test of a pre-production 310-horse Super Duty Trans Am. "How it ever got past the preview audience in GM's board room is a mystery, but here it is—the car that couldn't happen." Unfortunately it didn't stick around for long.

After building 300 Super Duty Firebirds for 1973, Pontiac sold only another 1,000 in 1974 before reality finally caught up this passionate Poncho. Although it did manage to slip by the smog police originally, the 455 Super Duty never would've been able to peacefully coexist with the catalytic converters to come. Its departure then for all signaled the end of the road for truly super supercar performance.

Was it a coincidence that the company that built the first great

A ducktail spoiler was again standard for the 1974 Trans Am, as it had been since 1970.

The 455 SD V8 (above) ran both clean and strong. Nonetheless, an 8,000-rpm tach (above right) was a bit optimistic.

SPECIFICATIONS

Wheelbase: 108 inches

Weight: 3,760 pounds

Base Price: $4,350

Engine: 455 cubic-inch LS2 "Super Duty" V8

Horsepower: 290 at 4,000 rpm

Torque: 395 at 3,200 rpm

Induction: single Rochester Quadra-Jet four-barrel carburetor

Transmission: Turbo 400 automatic transmission (four-speed manual also available)

Suspension: independent A-arms w/coil springs in front; live axle with leaf springs in back

Brakes: power front discs, rear drums

Performance: 14.25 seconds in the quarter-mile in 1974; 13.8 seconds for the quarter-mile (310-horse model) in 1973

Production: 943 (another 57 Super Duty Formula Firebirds were also built in 1974)

Fender-mounted air extractors became a Trans Am trademark in 1970 and remained standard until 1982.

1996 *Dodge Viper* GTS

The Corvette has long been known as "America's Sports Car," and probably always will be. Only one king can rule the road, and Chevrolet's 'glass-bodied two-seater has reigned supreme now for 50 years; its tenure alone guarantees a tough task for any car intending to unseat it. Sure, there have been pretenders to the thrown over the last half-century. But not one has actually dared to go toe-to-toe with the entrenched incumbent.

Ford's two-seat Thunderbirds from 1955-57? Though they were obvious knock-offs, they still represented a breed all their own, a species Dearborn officials like to call "personal luxury." More performance-oriented were the supercharged Studebakers of the Fifties, the blown Avanti (another Stude) in the Sixties, and American Motors' AMX, a two-seater that came in 1968 and went in '70. Nice tries all, but each was better off staying on its own familiar porch and letting Chevy's really big dog run wherever it wanted.

No so for Carroll Shelby's Ford-powered Cobras, built from 1962 to '68. Shelby American's crude 427 Cobra certainly could take a savage bite out of a big-block Corvette driver's lunch.

Below: *A sight to strike terror into your heart when this appears in your rear-view mirror.*

Nonetheless, Sting Rays continued owning the American road during the Sixties, thanks to, if nothing else, sheer numbers. Twenty-thousand Corvettes a year easily overshadowed the couple hundred Cobras let loose during their entire run. Additionally, cost, convenience and class were all clearly in Chevrolet's favor.

Much the same still could be said three decades down the road when Dodge rolled out its vicious Viper in 1992. Like the Corvette in its infancy, the Viper came into this world with little more than the four wheels it rolled in on. In both cases, a sloppy soft-top and side curtains didn't quite cut it with spoiled Yankees. Forty-seven years ago Chevrolet designers rectified their situation by introducing a new Corvette body with real roll-up side glass and an optional removable hardtop. Then in 1963 the Sting Ray coupe was unveiled to the delight of toupee-wearing sports car enthusiasts everywhere.

Thirty years later, Viper drivers were roughing it and not liking it much at all. Complaints about the open-air cockpit were just the beginning. Many critics also felt the Viper's original shin-sizzling sidepipes weren't too cool. They not only made entry and exit a lot like jumping from the frying pan into the fire, they also didn't do much at all for the way the aluminum V10 announced its presence. According to AutoWeek's Matt DeLorenzo, the original Viper RT/10 roadster sounded like "a UPS truck at idle."

Although Dodge officials knew that they too were in no way intending to "out-Corvette" the Corvette, they did have ears and eyes; they could hear those complaints and they could see the obvious solution. In 1995 they introduced a closed version of their wild and wooly RT/10 roadster to hopefully help soothe the ruffled feelings (and follicles) of potential buyers who felt the original Viper was just too damned uncivilized. That this slippery roof also improved aerodynamics and thus raised top end was simply icing on the cake. Or was it the other way around?

Labeled a 1996 model, the Viper GTS coupe represented the closest thing to a stab at sophistication for a car that already had made a name for itself as a brute-force beast. Along with its nicely styled-in hardtop, the GTS coupe also incorporated the breed's first real roll-up (electrically) windows, a more socially acceptable feature that then carried over into the Viper roadster's ranks. Although the already cramped passenger compartment was made even more foreboding with the low, fixed roof in place, at least designers managed to allow stature-challenged drivers a better fit behind the wheel. New for the GTS were adjustable foot pedals that could be mechanically moved four inches forward and backward. Dual airbags and better-located instruments were also included.

MILESTONE FACTS

- Dodge had a Viper prototype up and running in 1988. This red roadster then made its first public appearance on January 4, 1989.
- The Viper's V-10 engine came from Dodge's truck line.
- Dodge's Mitsubishi-based Stealth was initially chosen to pace the 1991 Indianapolis 500, but it was replaced by a pre-production Viper after a wave of complaints arose about a "Japanese car" pacing the All-American 500.
- Looking a lot like Shelby American's Dayton coupe was not necessarily a coincidence in the GTS's case. Carroll Shelby was one of the Viper's "founding four fathers. The other three were Bob Lutz, Francois Castaing and Tom Gale.
- Engineering goals for the GTS involved keeping weight at the same level as the RT/10 roadster. Adding the roof meant cutting pounds elsewhere—the GTS engine alone weighed 80 pounds less than its predecessor.
- The GTS coupe's V-10 used a lumpier cam, more compression (9.6:1, compared to 9:1), better-breathing heads, and revised exhausts to jump up from 415 horsepower all the way to 450.

Both adding the roof and a revised floor pan resulted in a much more structurally sound body, and this newfound firmness was accented with a little-less-stout suspension, making the ride a little less rude. And while the exhausts still traveled through the door sills—which still got hot and still wore a warning sticker saying so—they now led all the way back to the Kamm-back tail, where some critics say they released a note more pleasing to the horsepower hound's ears. As for appearances, all GTS coupes were initially done only in blue with white racing stripes—a combination copied directly from Shelby's victories Daytona coupes of 1964.

Don't kid yourself, however, the GTS coupe was no watered-down snake. Beneath that beautiful blue body went a lightened, pumped up version of the 8.0-liter V-10, which had been rated at 415 horsepower in previous roadster applications. Advertised output for the GTS was 450 horses, easily the most offered around Detroit in 1996.

More horsepower, more mph on top end, and more conveniences inside—could it get any better? Corvette customers might've thought so, but then maybe they had grown too soft. As far as sheer muscle was concerned, nothing beat a Viper GTS in 1996. At least nothing American.

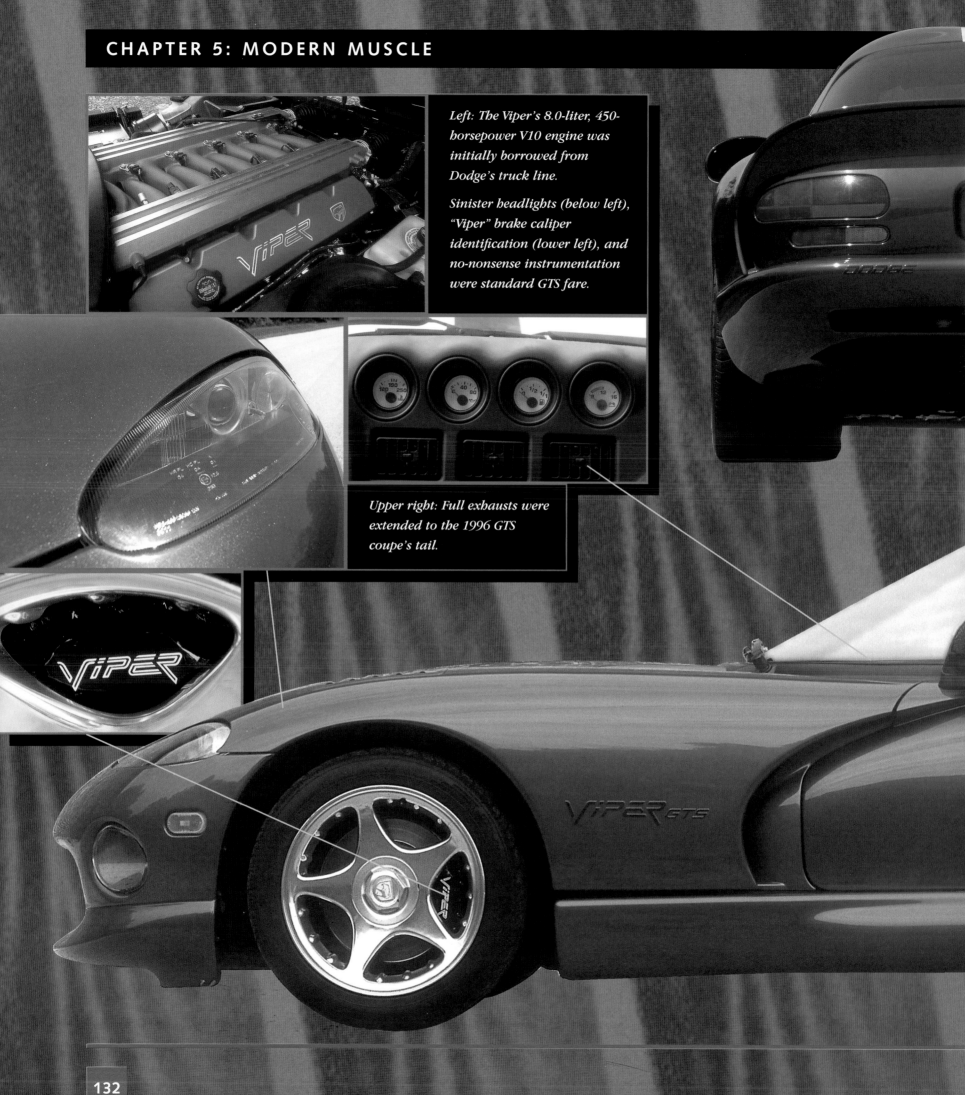

Left: The Viper's 8.0-liter, 450-horsepower V10 engine was initially borrowed from Dodge's truck line.

Sinister headlights (below left), "Viper" brake caliper identification (lower left), and no-nonsense instrumentation were standard GTS fare.

Upper right: Full exhausts were extended to the 1996 GTS coupe's tail.

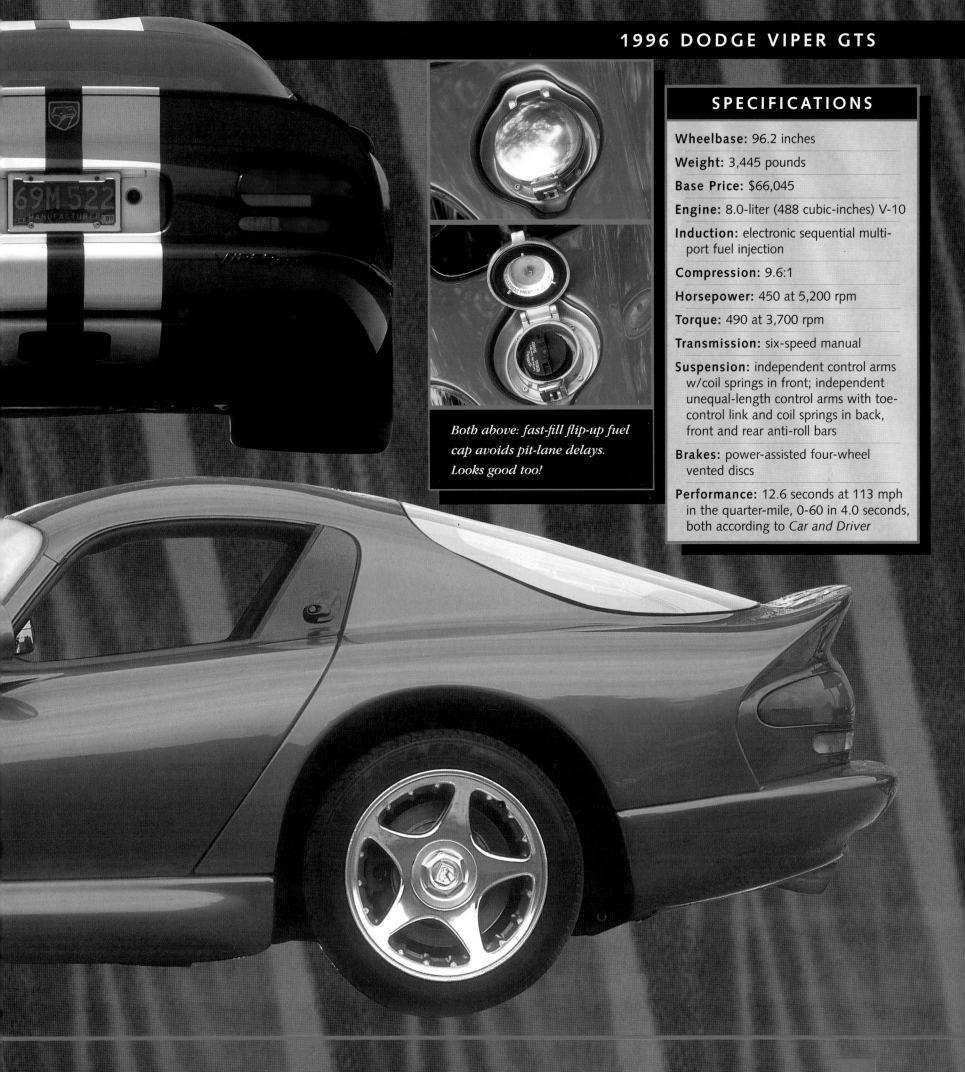

SPECIFICATIONS

Wheelbase: 96.2 inches

Weight: 3,445 pounds

Base Price: $66,045

Engine: 8.0-liter (488 cubic-inches) V-10

Induction: electronic sequential multi-port fuel injection

Compression: 9.6:1

Horsepower: 450 at 5,200 rpm

Torque: 490 at 3,700 rpm

Transmission: six-speed manual

Suspension: independent control arms w/coil springs in front; independent unequal-length control arms with toe-control link and coil springs in back, front and rear anti-roll bars

Brakes: power-assisted four-wheel vented discs

Performance: 12.6 seconds at 113 mph in the quarter-mile, 0-60 in 4.0 seconds, both according to *Car and Driver*

Both above: fast-fill flip-up fuel cap avoids pit-lane delays. Looks good too!

1996 *Chevy Camaro* Z28 SS

Chevrolet's Super Sport legacy goes back a long way and has involved various models (including a few pickups in more recent years) over that span. Introduced for the 1961 Impala, the way-cool SS package then showed up on the compact Nova (1963), the mid-sized Chevelle (1964), the F-body Camaro (1967), the split-personality El Camino (1968), and upscale Monte Carlo (1970).

By the Seventies, though, the good ol' Super Sport ideal was no longer such a big deal. The original, the full-sized Impala SS, was last seen in 1969, and Chevrolet product planners last stuck an SS badge on the 1972 Camaro before finally ending the string entirely.... Case closed? Not at all.

With the rebirth of the great American musclecar in the Eighties came a new wave of nostalgia among car buyers, many of whom still remembered the Detroit's previous horsepower race. Automakers in turn then fanned these flames of desire by offering more and more muscle during the Nineties. In 1992, a typical hot American V8 made about 205 horsepower. Within four years or so that bar had been raised to more the 300 horses. And along with the rise of those big ponies came the return of a familiar name.

In 1994 Chevrolet dusted off its Super Sport image and applied it, peculiarly enough, to a four-door Caprice. Presto, instant Impala SS, a nicely performing family car that rolled on until 1996. That same a year, another SS model reappeared, only it wasn't exactly Chevrolet's idea, though it was sold directly through Chevy dealerships.

Checking off regular production option number R7T in 1996 put a driver behind the wheel of a new Camaro Z28 SS, which actually was created by an outside contractor, SLP Engineering, Inc., in Troy, Michigan. SLP was the same firm that had started doing similar conversion for Pontiac in 1992, with the end result being the hopped-up Firehawk Firebird. After the Firehawk took flight, SLP then became to General Motors what SVT (Special Vehicle Team, creators of the Mustang Cobra) is to Ford.

A '96 SS began life like any other Z28 Camaro at GM's F-body plant in St. Therese, Quebec. When the R7T option was ordered, Chevrolet sent a Z/28 from St. Therese to an SLP shop in nearby Boisbriand, where it was treated to the Street Legal touch, all the while remaining emissions legal to the strictest U.S. standards. Also met were General Motors' tough standards.

MILESTONE FACTS

- Prior to 1996, Chevrolet last built a Camaro SS in 1972.
- SLP Engineering offered its SS conversion for Camaro Z28 coupes and convertibles in 1996.
- The Camaro Z28 SS debuted just as Chevrolet was shutting down its Caprice-based Impala SS.
- The "SLP" in SLP Engineering originally stood for "Street Legal Performance."
- "Premium floor mats" wearing a "Z28 SS" logo were an SLP option for the 1996 Camaro SS.
- According to Hot Rod's Drew Hardin, "the upgraded SS suspension virtually glued the Camaro to the road."

"Throughout the SS's development phase, our objective was to engineer the very highest quality vehicle," added SLP president Ed Hamburger in 1996. " In addition to offering world-class performance, another objective is to make the ownership process as easy as possible. For example, ordering a Z28 SS will be as simple as visiting your local Chevy dealer and asking for an order form''. SLP's basic makeover began with a bulging forced-air hood that helped boost the Z28's LT1 small-block from 285 horsepower to 310. Underneath went thicker anti-sway bars front and rear and a Panhard bar in back, all with stiffened bushings for added precision. Corvette ZR-1 17x9 cast-aluminum wheels wearing Z-rated Goodrich Comp T/A rubber went on at the corners. "SS" fender tags, a slightly revised rear spoiler, and numbered i.d. plate on the console completed the deal, which added about four-grand to a Z28's base sticker.

Like its Firehawk Firebird cousin, the Camaro SS offered F-body buyers a chance at supreme F-body performance at a cost that wasn't all that tough to stomach. Sure handling, souped-up LT1 power, truly tough looks—what else would you expect from a great American musclecar?

SPECIFICATIONS

Wheelbase: 101.1 inches

Weight: 4,365 pounds

Base price: $24,500

Engine: 350 cubic-inch LT1 V8 with iron block, aluminum heads

Induction: electronic sequential-port fuel injection

Compression: 10.4:1

Horsepower: 310 at 5,500 rpm

Torque: 325 at 2,400 rpm

Transmission: Borg-Warner T56 six-speed manual

Suspension: independent A-arms w/coil springs in front; live axle with coil springs torque arms, trailing arms and tack bar in back

Brakes: four-wheel vented discs

Performance: 13.5 seconds at 104.86 mph in quarter-mile, according to *Hot Rod*

Production: 2,410

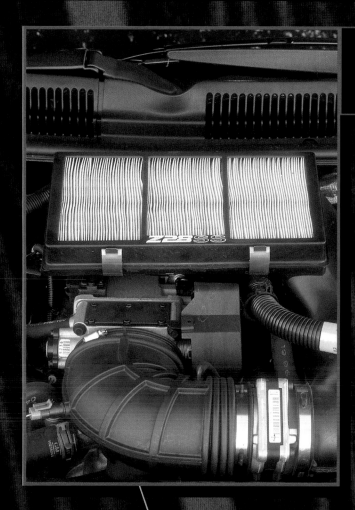

Left: SLP enhancements boosted the LT1 small-block V8's output to 310 horsepower.

The Camaro Z28 SS debuted just as Chevrolet's reborn Impala SS was retiring.

A numbered i.d. plate (far left) was standard inside, as were Corvette wheels (left) at the corners.

Below: "SS" badging and a bold ram-air hood were trademarks of the SLP-tweaked Camaro.

1999 Pontiac Trans Am
30th Anniversary Edition

Most casual witnesses who witnessed Pontiac's 30th Anniversary Trans Am Firebird in 1999 couldn't have helped having an opinion. Gray area didn't exist; they either loved the car or not. Those residing down at the "nay" end of the scale, those who weren't tickled white and blue all over, had the same basic complaint: they simply couldn't stomach those wheels.

Indeed, from a Nineties perspective when ever-trendy monochromatic appeals dominated, those metallic blue rims did tend to stick out in stark contrast to that blinding white finish.

Ah, but therein awaited the rub. Call them garish if you will, but those wheels had to be there, they belonged on the car. Like the legendary "screaming chicken" that had been hanging around T/A hoods since 1973, those somewhat radioactive rims shouted out

"Trans Am" in no uncertain terms. The color combo choice itself was obvious. All of those first Trans Am Firebirds way back in 1969 were painted the same: Cameo White adorned by Lucerne Blue racing stripes. But commemorating the exclusive color treatment

Below: *Pontiac celebrated 30 uninterrupted years of Trans Ams in 1999 with a special-anniversary model (at left). At right is a 1969 T/A.*

applied 30 years ago was one thing, carrying on in a rich, high-flying tradition of high-profile performance was another.

That the '99 30th Anniversary Trans Am stood out from the crowd so prominently even while at rest is exactly what Pontiac Motor Division's free-thinking builders of excitement had in mind—color-conscious critics be damned. Pontiac wanted to wake people up, something Trans Ams had been doing with little respect for teetotaler's tastes and puritanical customs longer than any other American heavy-metal out there. Remember, Chevrolet's 50-year-old Corvette is made of plastic, not steel. Well, maybe there was a lot of plastic compound in the 1999 Trans Am, too, but you get the picture.

There also was a lot of purebred muscle in there thanks to the inclusion of a slightly detuned version of the C5 Corvette's 5.7-liter LS1 V8. The LS1's 320 romping, stomping horses helped keep the 30th Anniversary Trans Am at the head of the modern musclecar pack, a familiar place for Pontiac's F-body bloodline. PMD people in 1999 were more than proud of the fact that the Trans Am was

then the only musclecar (again remember, the Corvette is technically "America's Sports Car") able to lay claim to a continuous run dating back to the good ol' days of unbridled horsepower. While Chevrolet briefly gave up on the long-running F-body performance machine, the Z/28 Camaro, in the late-Seventies, Pontiac planners kept their hottest Firebird running even through the darkest days. Safety crusaders, clean-air cops, Arab oil sheiks—no one could stop the Trans Am.

Pontiac offered its 30th Anniversary Trans Am in both coupe and convertible form. Along with that exclusive paint scheme and those blue rims, all the 30th Anniversary models were also fitted with the warmly welcomed "WS6" Ram-Air hood, a feature that looked great and worked even greater to free a few extra ponies on the top

MILESTONE FACTS

- Until GM's recent cancellation of its F-body line, Pontiac's Firebird Trans Am was the only musclecar (save for America's Sports Car, the Corvette) to run uninterrupted from its birth in the Sixties into the new millennium.

- Special-edition anniversary Trans Am packages also appeared in 1979 (10th), 1984 (15th), 1989 (20th) and 1994 (25th).

- Production of 30th Anniversary Trans Ams, both coupes and convertibles, was limited to 1,600.

- Pontiac's 25th Anniversary Trans Am in 1994 also featured an exclusive blue-on-white finish. Its production was limited to 2,000.

- General Motors' recent cancellation of its F-body (Pontiac Firebird, Chevrolet Camaro) platform may well translate into soaring collector-car values for all of Pontiac's anniversary Trans Am models.

end. Behind that free-breathing LS1 V8 was a choice of either a four-speed automatic or six-speed manual transmission. As for those "medium-blue-tinted clearcoat" wheels, they were big 17x9 five-spokes fitted with P275/40ZR-17 rubber. Underneath was Pontiac's performance and handling package. Power-assisted four-wheel ABS disc brakes were standard, as was a special cooler for the power steering pump.

Inside, white leather buckets carried special "30th Anniversary" embroidery on their headrests, and anniversary identification also appeared on the floor mats and door panels. All cars also received an individually number plaque on the console. And convertibles were topped with an exclusive Medium Navy Blue cloth top.

Built with loyal collectors in mind, the 30th Anniversary followed in the limited-edition tracks of earlier commemorative Trans Ams. Save for the 10th Anniversary model of 1979 (7,500 built), no other birthday-marking Firebird sold more than 2,000 copies. Only 1,500 were sold in 1984, 1,555 in 1989 and the aforementioned two-grand in 1994. Only 1,600 1999 renditions were projected. As Firebird brand manager Tom Murray told Musclecar Review magazine's Dan Burger in 1999, "we kept the production numbers small so the ones that are out there will be that much more valuable."

Now that the Firebird family itself is history, those values should be taking off soon. The Trans Am may be gone, but it never will be forgotten.

Special identification carried over inside to the 30th Anniversary Tran Am's bucket seat headrests.

Above: Pontiac's WS6 ram-air equipment included an aggressive hood with twin scoops.

1999 30TH ANNIVERSARY PONTIAC TRANS AM

Left: A numbered console plaque also was included as part of the deal.

Right: At the time, the 1999 Trans Am was America's longest-running musclecar.

SPECIFICATIONS

Wheelbase: 101.1 inches

Weight: 3,474 pounds

Base Price: $35,495

Engine: 5.7-liter (346 cubic inches) V8 with aluminum block and heads

Induction: electronic-controlled sequential-port fuel injection with "WS6" Ram Air hood

Compression: 10.5:1

Horsepower: 320 at 5,200 rpm

Torque: 335 at 4,400 rpm

Transmission: four-speed automatic, standard; six-speed manual, optional

Suspension: independent short/long arms w/coil springs in front; live axle with coil springs, torque arms and track bar in back.

Brakes: power four-wheel discs

Production: 1,600 in 1999; 1,065 coupes, 535 convertibles

The 30th Anniversary Tran Am's standard bright blue wheels represented a love 'em or hate 'em proposition.

2001 *Chevy Corvette* Z06

Both critics and company officials alike couldn't say enough about the new "C5" (for 5th generation) Corvette after it hit the ground running in 1997. Practically no bolt had been left unturned by David Hill's engineering team when it had come time to reinvent America's Sports Car, resulting in a truly new Corvette from head to toe, from top to bottom.

The exciting LS1 V8 up front. A unique transmission/transaxle in back. An innovative, more rigid frame (formed by water pressure) underneath. The list went on and on. Improved comfort and convenience combined with the best world-class Vette performance yet, and all this at a reasonable price as American as apple pie. Could it get any better?

Yes, at least from an enthusiastic road-warrior's perspective.

In the C5, Hill's gang had America's all-time best musclecar, the most well-rounded performer to ever roll down Mainstreet U.S.A. Viper fans could forget about it. Though their new Dodge GTS coupe certainly was hotter than hot, it simply couldn't

Right: *Chevrolet introduced its supreme Corvette, the Z06, in 2001.*

compare to the C5 Corvette as far as real-world user-friendliness was concerned. On top of that its price tag was more than 50 percent higher. Case closed.

But Hill knew that not all Corvette customers wanted the best of both worlds, performance and practicality. Some didn't mind riding on the wild side with the Viper clan, they didn't worry about making

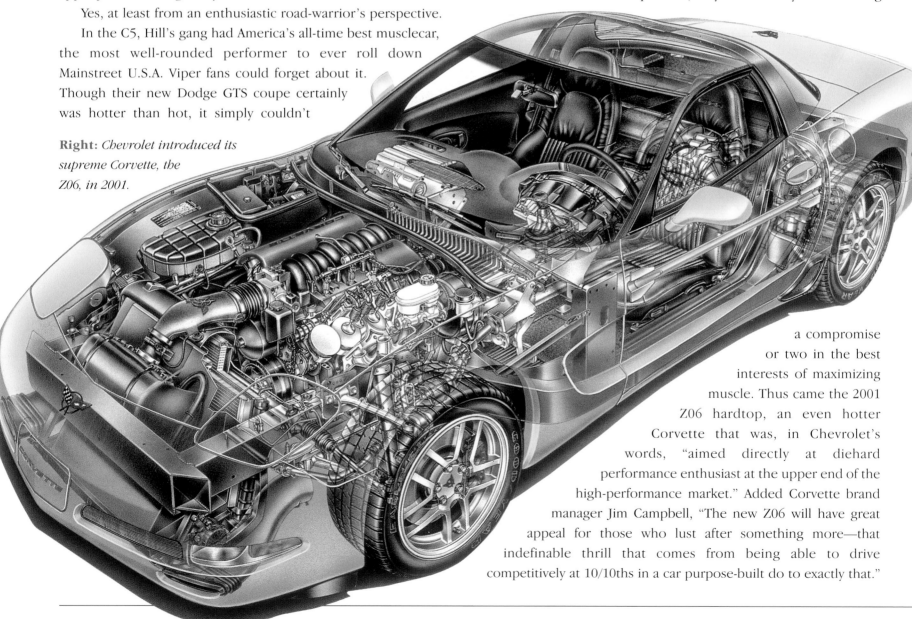

a compromise or two in the best interests of maximizing muscle. Thus came the 2001 Z06 hardtop, an even hotter Corvette that was, in Chevrolet's words, "aimed directly at diehard performance enthusiast at the upper end of the high-performance market." Added Corvette brand manager Jim Campbell, "The new Z06 will have great appeal for those who lust after something more—that indefinable thrill that comes from being able to drive competitively at 10/10ths in a car purpose-built do to exactly that."

Once more, few bolts went untouched as engineers created the Z06 hardtop, which borrowed its name from another hot Corvette, this one created by Zora Arkus-Duntov in 1963. Duntov's original Z06 options package included the new Sting Ray's hottest V8 working in concert with a beefed suspension and brakes to help make a trip from the showroom right to the racetrack possible. The plan was similar in 2001. Standard for the second-edition Z06 were wider wheels and tires, special brake-cooling ductwork front and rear, and the exclusive FE4 suspension, which featured a larger

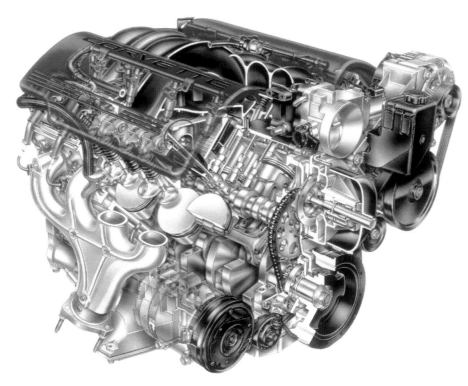

Above: *Powering the reborn Z06 in 2001 was the 385-horse LS6 V8.*

front stabilizer bar, a stiffer leaf spring in back, and revised camber settings at both ends. Weight was cut throughout the Z06 by about 100 pounds overall compared to a 2001 Corvette sport coupe.

The Z06's exclusive wheels were 17x9.5 inchers in front, 18x10.5 in back—in both cases one inch wider than the standard C5 rims. Mounted on the Z06's widened rollers were Goodyear Eagle F1 SC tires, P265/40ZR-17 in front, P295/35ZR-18 in back. C5s in 2001 featured Eagle F1 GS rubber, P245/45ZR-17 at the nose, P275/40ZR-18 at the tail.

Beneath the new Z06's hood was another hot power source, this one created only for this application. And, like the car itself, this exclusive engine was named using a legendary options code from Corvette days gone by. In 1971, the LS6 454 big-block was the

MILESTONE FACTS

- All C5 Corvettes in 1997 were targa-top sport coupes. A convertible joined the C5 line in 1998, and a fixed-roof hardtop followed in 1999.
- All Z06 Corvettes in 2001 were hardtop models. The LS6 V8 was exclusive to the Z06, while all other Corvettes came standard with the LS1 engine.
- Production of Corvette sport coupes and convertibles in 2001 was 15,681 and 14,173, respectively.
- Z06 colors in 2001 were Quicksilver Metallic, Speedway White, black, Torch Red, and Millennium Yellow.
- Only two interior colors were offered for the 2001 Z06, black and black w/Torch Red accents.
- Z06 tachometers redlined at 6,500 rpm, compared to 6,000 on other Corvettes.
- Chevrolet's second-generation active handling package was standard on all 2001 Corvettes.
- The M12 six-speed manual transmission and FE4 suspension were both exclusive to the 2001 Z06.

hottest Corvette V8 offered that year. Same for the 2001 LS6, which was based on the C5's existing LS1 small-block. A recast block, stronger pistons, raised compression (from 10.1 to 10.5:1), a lumpier cam, and bigger injectors were just a few of the dozens of LS 6 improvements. Output was 385 horsepower, 40 more than the LS1. Behind the LS6 was a new M12 six-speed manual transmission, the only gearbox available for the Z06.

These new parts and many others helped make the Z06, again in Chevrolet's words, "simply the quickest, best handling production Corvette ever." "We've enhanced Corvette's performance persona and broken new ground with the new Z06," added David Hill. "With 0-60 [times] of four seconds flat, and more than 1g of cornering acceleration, the Z06 truly takes Corvette performance to the next level. In fact, the Corvette Team has begun referring to it as the C5.5, so marked are the improvements we've made and the optimization of the car in every dimension."

Chevrolet sold 5,773 Z06 Corvettes in 2001, followed by another 8,297 in 2002. Continued popularity in 2003 proved that David Hill wasn't just trying to ride Duntov's coattails when he reached back to 1963 for a suitable name for his latest, greatest C5.

Zora undoubtedly would be proud.

Below: Z06 nomenclature was first seen on Corvette order sheets in 1963.

Right: Comfort and convenience were enhanced inside the C5 Corvette, introduced for 1997.

SPECIFICATIONS

Wheelbase: 104.5 inches

Weight: 3,115 pounds

Base Price: $47,500

Engine: 5.7-liter (346 cubic inches) LS6 V8 with aluminum block and heads

Induction: electronic sequential fuel injection

Compression: 10.5:1

Horsepower: 385 at 6,000 rpm

Torque: 385 at 4,800 rpm

Transmission: six-speed manual, located at rear wheels

Suspension: independent double wishbone w/coil springs in front; independent with cast-aluminum upper control arms and transverse-mounted composite leaf spring

Brakes: power-assisted four-wheel discs w/Bosch ABS

Performance: 12.6 seconds at 114 mph in the quarter-mile, 171-mph top speed (factory test)

Production: 5,773

The 2001-edition LS6 V8 featured aluminum block and heads.

2003 *Ford Mustang* Mach 1

Unlike their counterparts at General Motors, Ford officials haven't been all that keen on nostalgic commemorations in recent years. Nary a balloon or birthday candle was seen when Dearborn's beloved ponycar turned 30, perhaps because Ford execs felt totally redesigning the 1994 Mustang was enough.

Not even a simple anniversary badge appeared. And when humble logos did appear on the 35th Mustang in 1999, that adornment paled in comparison to what Pontiac did to celebrate 30 years of Trans Am Firebirds that same year. Chevrolet's 30th Anniversary Camaro had been honored with equal enthusiasm two years before.

But apparently some of the Blue Oval boys (and girls) do have hearts, they can relate to fond memories of days gone by. Or perhaps someone at Ford simply decided to copy what Chevrolet had done in 2001 with its Z06 Corvette. Either way, the end result was a special-edition ponycar for 2003 that harked back to 1969, the

year Ford designers unveiled what Car Life magazine editors called "the first great Mustang." That machine was the Mach 1, which—again in Car Life's words—offered "performance to match its looks, handling to send imported-car fans home mumbling to themselves, and an interior as elegant, and livable, as a gentleman's club."

Indeed, the idea behind the first Mach 1 was to combine a little class and a bit of prestige with a decent dose of performance, or at least a decent performance image. Base small-block Mach 1 fastbacks looked great in 1969, but weren't all that hot. On the contrary, the optional 428 Cobra Jet big-block V8—fit with Ford's new "Shaker" ram-air hood scoop—instantly transformed the

upscale Mustang into "the quickest standard passenger car though the quarter-mile we've ever tested," according to Car Life's critics, this after a stunning 13.86-second quarter-mile sprint.

It was this legacy of performance and pizzazz that Ford product planners tapped into 24 years later. They already had a decent all-around "hi-po" hauler in the Mustang GT, a nicely affordable thoroughly modern musclecar that offered even more comfort and convenience than that first Mach 1. Ford buyers in 2003 could also opt for the pricier SVT Cobra, back after a one-year hiatus with 390 supercharged horses. Yet in between was a major gap. No problem. Those planners simply filled that hole with the 2003 Mach 1, a Mustang that looked an awful lot like a time machine.

First and foremost there was that familiar Shaker scoop protruding up through the '03 Mach 1's striped hood. Like its fully functional forerunner, this black baby could rock like Mick Jagger when the torque started twisting. "Let your mind go and it's the Sixties all over the place," wrote Hot Rod's Ro McGonegal about that new old-style scoop. Doing that twisting was a 2003 redo of the 2001 Cobra's 4.6-liter dual-overhead-cam, four-valve-per-cylinder V8, a 305-horse screamer that made the latest, greatest Mach 1 even faster than its big-block ancestor. It also made the 2003 Mach 1 the first Mustang outside of the SVT corral to offer DOHC V8 power.

The new Mach 1 could out-handle its forefather, too, thanks to a special suspension package that featured stiffer springs (that lowered the car about a half inch), Tokico struts, and 17x8 wheels shod in Goodyear Eagle ZR45 rubber. Those aluminum five-spoke "Heritage" wheels were unique to the 2003 Mach 1 and fit the nostalgic image to a T, as did those blacked-out front rear spoilers and those old-fashioned rocker panel stripes. Fog lamps too were standard up front, per GT specs.

Additional standard equipment included a Tremec five-speed manual transmission,

Left: *Ford revived its revered Mach 1 moniker in 2003 to help mark the corporation's 100th anniversary.*

MILESTONE FACTS

- Ford's original Mach 1 Mustang debuted for 1969 as an upscale fastback.
- The original "Shaker" hood scoop option was offered atop various engines between Mustang flanks in 1969 and '70. It also peeked through the Torino Cobra hoods in 1970 and '71.
- Ford called its new Mach 1 Mustang a "modern interpretation of an American icon."
- Production breakdown by transmission choice for the 2003 Mach 1 was 7,709 manuals, 1,943 automatics. The 2003 Mach 1 was the first Mustang to mate Ford's 4.6-liter DOHC V8 with an automatic transmission.
- Production breakdown by exterior color was 2,513 for Torch Red, 2,250 for Azure Blue, 1,611 for black, 1,595 for Dark Shadow Grey, 869 for Zinc Yellow, and 814 for Oxford White
- Two new Mach 1 colors were introduced for the 2004 model year, Screaming Yellow and Competition Orange. Commemorative identification, marking the Mustang's 40th anniversary, was also added.

power rack-and-pinion steering, power four-wheel Brembo disc brakes, stainless-steel dual exhausts, and a Trac-Lok 8.8-inch differential with 3.55:1 gears. A beefed-up 4R70W automatic transmission was optional.

Ordering the automatic required a few changes within the DOHV V8. Crankshafts in auto-box engines were cast pieces, while their counterparts in stick-shift Mach 1s were forged steel. Output ratings remained the same, but redlines differed—5,800 revs in automatic cars versus a grand more in the manuals. Additional 4.6L DOHC updates in 2003 (in both cases) included revised cylinder heads with rerouted water passages, new cams (the intake valves were controlled by a bumpstick borrowed from Ford's 5.4L truck engine), and revamped exhaust manifolds that were port-matched to the heads.

Standard interior treatments also brought back memories as the Mach 1 was fitted with a bright aluminum shift "ball" and a "nostalgic instrument cluster," both features that had appeared previously on Ford's "Bullitt" Mustang. Indeed, it was the Sixties all over again when seated at a 2003 Mach 1's leather-wrapped wheel looking past those gauges over that black scoop that quivered with every bit as much as excitement as the driver.

All that was missing was an SS 396 Chevelle or Hemi Road Runner in the lane next door.

SPECIFICATIONS

Wheelbase: 101.3 inches

Weight: 3,465 pounds

Base Price: $28,805

Engine: 4.6-liter dual-overhead-cam V8 with four-valves per cylinder

Induction: electronic sequential fuel injection with 57mm throttle body and functional "Shaker" hood scoop

Compression: 10.1:1

Horsepower: 305 at 5,800 rpm

Torque: 320 at 4,200 rpm

Transmission: Tremec TR3650 five-speed manual (automatic optionals)

Suspension: independent A-arms w/coil springs in front; live axle with coil springs in back

Brakes: power four-wheel discs

Performance: 12.97 seconds at 103 mph in the quarter-mile, according to Mustang Monthly

Production: 9,652

Ford musclecar fans recognized the Mach 1's "shaker" hood scoop (left), which fed cooler outside air to a 305-horse 4.6-liter V8. Nostalgic touches inside (right) included "Bullitt" Mustang instruments, foot pedals and shifter knob.

The shaker scoop and striping (above) were all plainly reminiscent of Ford's first-generation Mach 1. This well-known badge (right) first appeared in 1969.

2004 Pontiac GTO

It was only right that the same firm that ushered in the musclecar era in 1964 also ended things 10 years later. In nearly all opinions, Pontiac's GTO was America's first muscle machine, and many feel the division's 455 Super Duty Firebird, built in 1973 and '74, was the last. The last truly great one, that is.

From then on, it was Pontiac's Trans Am or nothing at all as far as most typical (translated: those who couldn't afford a Corvette) performance fans were concerned back in the horsepower-starved Seventies and Eighties. Though these "T/A" Firebirds basically represented mere shadows of their former selves, at least they stuck around every year, unlike their F-body cousin from Chevy, the Z28 Camaro. Then once real factory muscle started making its comeback some 20 years back, the long-running Trans Am was ready, willing

and able to really start rolling again. Unfortunately GM's last F-body rolled into the sunset in 2002, leaving Pontiac without a traditional rear-driven V8 musclecar for the first time since… well, since 1964.

No worries, mate. Built in Australia, Pontiac's newest pumped-up sport coupe picked up where the Trans Am left off and hit the

Below: *The Tiger is back! Pontiac reintroduced its famed GTO for 2004 after a 30-year hiatus.*

ground running on the U.S. market in 2004 to rave reviews, both from contemporary critics with no "original" musclecar experience as well as those who lived it the first time around. The name alone was enough to stir the soul: GTO. Who cares that the car beneath that famous three-letter badge is a warmed-up version of General Motors' Aussie-marketed Holden Monaro, first seen at the Sydney motor show in 1998? It's a two-door coupe, it's suitably muscular, and it's certainly better than, say, nothing.

By then based on Pontiac's compact Ventura, the last original GTO had come and gone in 1974, looking more like a feeble farewell than a suitably honorable send-off for a legendary automobile. Rumors of a return began surfacing 20-odd years later, but these initially were nothing more than teases.

"We considered bringing the GTO back a number of times, but we never had the right product," explained Pontiac-GMC general manager Lynn Myers in January 2003. "We knew it had to be a V8, rear-wheel drive and offer outstanding performance, but, until GM's leadership team looked at the Holden Monaro, nothing really fit."

Though looking to GM's affiliate Down Under might not have been the prime choice, Pontiac execs were undoubtedly pressured into a relatively painless plan of least resistance once word came down of the F-body's impending doom. Replacing the retiring Trans Am with a new GTO became that plan, but it had to be put in place fast, thus the use of the existing Holden platform. From first suggestion to production reality amazingly required only 17 months.

"The speed to market with the new GTO demonstrates GM's global product development capabilities and our renewed focus on customer enthusiasm," added Bob Lutz, GM vice chairman of product development and the former Chrysler man who had previously shepherded in Dodge's Viper. "This car is a strong statement from both Pontiac and GM that we are determined to re-energize the car market with vehicles that command attention and excite the customer's senses."

The main source of the new GTO's excitement is its LS1 V8, which has been the heart of the Corvette since the C5 debuted in 1997. Rated at 350 horsepower, the 2004 GTO's LS1 is mated to a standard 4L60-E automatic transmission, which can be superseded by an optional close-ratio Tremec six-speed manual (the same gearbox used by the Z06 Corvette) for those who prefer to row their own way through the gears.

Additional standard hardware includes power-assisted four-

MILESTONE FACTS

- Pontiac's original GTO was built from 1964 to 1974. Nearly 515,000 "Goats" hit the streets during that time.

- From 1964 to '68, GTO was America's best-selling musclecar.

- For 1974 only, the GTO was based on the compact Ventura platform. It had been a mid-sized model prior to that point.

- Pontiac got enthusiasts hopes up in 1999 with a GTO concept car, which was actually an inoperative foam model that, in the words of Car and Driver's Aaron Robinson, "was too ugly even for Hot Wheels to build."

- According to Car and Driver, the 2004 GTO represents "God-bless-America performance wrapped in a sleek and refined package at a price the rest of us can afford."

- Reportedly Pontiac's initial plans involve building about 18,000 GTOs a year for three years.

- Pontiac's 2004 GTO was introduced at the Detroit and Los Angeles auto shows in January 2003. Production began late that year.

wheel ventilated disc brakes (with a four-channel anti-lock system), four-wheel independent suspension, power rack-and-pinion steering, and 17x8 cast aluminum wheels wearing BF Goodrich 245/45ZR-17 tires. Throw on some spoilers, appropriate "GTO" identification inside and out, and cool instrumentation and comfortable buckets within the cockpit and the deal's done. For about $33,000, a muscle-minded buyer can put himself (or herself) back behind the wheel of the car that started it all so many years ago.

Or at least something close to it. Though some critics early on have complained that the new Australian-born image fails to honor the old all-American Goat, the 2004 rendition's performance speaks for itself: 0-60 in 5.3 seconds, the quarter-mile in 13.62 clicks. Those numbers represent muscle enough for most drivers, and there's talk that Pontiac has an even hotter GTO in the works, a reborn "Judge" if you will. Offered from 1969 to '71, the original GTO Judge laid down the law in its day like few other factory hot rods. Will a similarly maxed-out GTO be back out in front again? At this point, the jury's still out.

In the meantime we do have yet another high-powered time machine, another new-wave musclecar that both revives fond memories and holds its own "in the now." Accord to Bob Lutz, "this latest GTO will carry on the proud tradition of a legendary line."

Hopefully it will also lead the way into a fast and furious future.

SPECIFICATIONS

Wheelbase: 109.7 inches

Weight: 3,821 pounds

Base Price: $33,000 (estimated)

Engine: 5.7-liter (346 cubic inches) LS1 pushrod V8 with aluminum block and heads

Induction: electronic sequential-port fuel injection

Compression: 10.1:1

Horsepower: 340 at 5,200 rpm

Torque: 360 at 4,000 rpm

Transmission: six-speed manual or four-speed Hydra-Matic automatic

Suspension: independent A-arms w/coil spring struts in front; live axle with coils springs, trailing arms and adjustable toe-in link in back

Brakes: four-wheel ventilated discs w/ABS

Performance: 13.62 seconds at 104.78 mph in the quarter-mile, according to Motor Trend test of six-speed manual model

Production (projected): 18,000

Standard muscle for the 2004 GTO is supplied by the 5.7-liter LS1 V8. Output is 340 horsepower.

Eye-catching instrumentation (above) and "GTO"-identified buckets (above left) are standard for the reborn "Goat." Buyers can choose between a six-speed manual (far left) or an automatic transmission.

Musclecar Timeline

1955 The first of Chrysler's hemi-powered "letter-series" 300 models appear. Chevrolet introduces the "Hot One," its new overhead-valve V8 model. The Corvette gets its first V8

1956 Chevrolet adds optional dual four-barrel carbs to its small-block V8. Plymouth introduced its limited-edition Fury, DeSoto its Adventurer, and Dodge its D-500, high-performance cars all.

1958 Chrysler kills its original hemi-head V8 in favor of lighter, easier-to-engineer wedge-head engines. Chevrolet introduces its first "W-head" V8, the 348, the forerunner to the fabled 409.

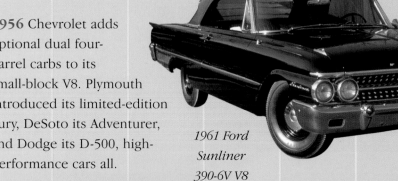

1961 Ford Sunliner 390-6V V8

1960 Ford gets back into the high-performance race with its 360-horse 352 Police Interceptor V8.

1955 Chrysler C-300

1961 Chevrolet's 409 V8 and Impala Super Sport debut. The Beach Boys' hit single, "409" storms the charts the following year.

1962 Carroll Shelby begins building Ford-powered Cobra in Southern California. Max Wedge Mopar super-stocks debut. Pontiac Super Duty Catalinas dominate NASCAR racing.

1963 Henry Ford II attempts to buy Ferrari but fails. General Motors execs order all divisions to cease racing activities. Chevrolet extends its sporty SS options group down into its compact Chevy II line. Dodge and Plymouth's Max Wedge V8 goes from 413 cubic-inches to 426.

1964 Ford Mustang ushers in "ponycar" era. Mustang convertible paces Indy 500. Pontiac ushers in musclecar era with its GTO. Oldsmobile's 4-4-2 debuts midyear. Chrysler Corporation revives Hemi power, but for racing only.

1966 A limited-edition special in 1965, Chevrolet's SS 396 is toned down (translated: priced right) and becomes an instant mass-market hit. Dodge and Plymouth's "street Hemi" debuts and never looks back.

1967 Chevrolet Camaro, Pontiac Firebird and Mercury Cougar debut. All offer optional big-block performance. The Trans-Am-inspired Z/28 Camaro also hits the street. Chevy builds 20 race-only L88 Corvettes.

1959 Pontiac's Super Duty parts program gets rolling despite the AMA ban on factory racing involvement. Ford announces it will begin offering performance parts after following the AMA edict tot he letter for two years.

1957 Chevrolet and Pontiac begin offering optional fuel-injection. Ford announces optional supercharging, but cancels this engine after the Automobile Manufacturers Association "bans" factory-backed racing projects.

300 horses were standard for the 1955 C-300

Custom wheelcover option for 1964 GTO

1965 Carroll Shelby introduces his GT-350 Shelby Mustang. Chevrolet's 396-cube Mk IV big-block makes the scene, opening the door for one of Detroit's most successful musclecars, the SS 396 Chevelle. Last Chrysler "letter-car," the 300L, is built.

1968	1969	1970	1971	1972	1973	1974	1975	1976	1977	1978	1979	1980

1969 Henry Ford II fires Bunkie Knudsen. Chevrolet's SS 396 Chevelle supersedes Pontiac's GTO as America's best-selling musclecar. Pontiac, meanwhile, rolls out its first Trans Am Firebird.

1969 Yenko Camaro

1974 Pontiac builds final GTO and last 455 Super Duty Firebird, the latter considered by many to be Detroit's last truly great musclecar. Last big-block Corvette built. Chevrolet temporarily discontinues its Z28 Camaro.

1978 Henry Ford II fires Lee Iacocca. Iacocca then heads straight for Chrysler, where he later brings old pal Carroll Shelby into the fold. Ford unveils its King Cobra Mustang II—disco fans love it.

1972 Stage 1 Buick and W30 Olds remain as able competitors in the weakened musclecar race. Chevrolet kills off its LT-1 Corvette at year's end.

1976 Cadillac's Eldorado ragtop said to be America's last convertible. Topless travel then resumes in force seven years later. Trans Am production at Pontiac jumps to nearly 47,000—no other choices out there.

1973 Energy crisis results after Organization of Petroleum Exporting Countries (OPEC) cut back oil delivers to West in protest of U.S. support of Israel. Pontiac's 455 Super Duty passes federal emissions muster despite its brutish nature.

1979 Redesigned Fox-chassis Mustang paces Indy 500. Little else to report.

1969 Pontiac Tran Am

Below: grill badge, of a 1970 Buick GTS

1970 Henry Ford II shuts down nearly all of his companies motorsport activities. Lee Iacocca becomes Ford president. Both the Boss 302 and Boss 429 Mustangs are gone by year's end after debuting in 1969.

Ford's Boss 429 Mustang and its huge hood scoop (above)

1971 Compression cuts, mandated by tighter federal emissions standards to come, being across the board in Detroit. By the end of the year all the great musclecar big-block V8s are cancelled.

1975 Chevrolet ends production of Corvette convertibles. Pontiac builds 27,274 Trans Am Firebirds, the only real musclecar (discounting the Corvette) left.

1977 Chevy's Z28 Camaro returns midyear. Another production leap for Pontiac's Trans Am, this time to nearly 69,000.

1980 Ford's Special Vehicle Operations (SVO) formed. Pontiac offers optional turbocharged V8 for Firebird models. Again, little else to report.

1968 Former GM exec Semon E. "Bunkie" Knudsen hired as Ford president. Ford's new 428 Cobra Jet Mustang shows big-block Camaros and Firebirds what for. New Dodge Charger body copies some of its essence from the equally new Corvette. Plymouth introduces its Road Runner.

1981 **1982** **1983** **1984** **1985** **1986** **1987** **1988** **1989** **1990** **1991** **1992** **1993**

1981 Last four-speed Corvette built until 1984.

1982 Chevrolet begins offering its "Cross Fire Injection" system for both its Corvette and Camaro.

1985 Ford begins bolting up real tube headers and true dual exhausts (with twin catalytic converters) to its 5.0L small-block, pumping output up to 210 horsepower.

1988 Chevrolet offers 35th Anniversary Corvette. Chevy's IROC-Z Camaro takes the place of long-running the Z28.

1989 Prototype ZR-1 Corvette wows musclecar crowd; regular-production version debuts for 1990. Chevrolet puts together its "1LE" performance package for its Camaro—only 111 are built.

1984 Ford introduces its SVO Mustang with turbocharged four-cylinder power. Both Ford and Pontiac build special commemorative models marking 20 years of Mustangs, 15 of Trans Ams, respectively. All-new Corvette debuts.

1987 Buick teams up with ASC/McLaren to produce the truly hot GNX with its turbocharged 3.8-liter V6. Rest to 60 mph for the GNX required only 5.5 seconds.

1990 Chevrolet builds 62 "1LE" Camaro coupes aimed at SCCA Showroom Stock racing.

1991 Chevrolet's Z28 Camaro returns as IROC-Z run ended in 1990. Another 478 "1LE" Camaros hit the streets.

Nothing seen in the Eighties could compare to the 455 SD Trans Am, last built in 1974

1986 Last SVO Mustang built. Corvette convertible returns just in time to pace the Indianapolis 500.

1983 Chevrolet fails to build a Corvette for the first time since 1953. Mustang convertible returns after 10-year hiatus.

Pontiac's 455 Super Duty V8 was the last great musclecar mill

1992 Dodge Viper debuts in roadster form only. Former Ford man Carroll Shelby contributed to Viper development. SLP, in Troy, Michigan, begins its Firehawk Firebird conversions for Pontiac

Anything that can be written to fill tis awkard space please!!!!

1993 Chevrolet offers 40th Anniversary Corvette. Ford's Special Vehicle Team (SVT) introduces its Cobra Mustang and Lightning pickup truck.

1994 | 1995 | 1996 | 1997 | 1998 | 1999 | 2000 | 2001 | 2002 | 2003 | 2004 | 2005 | 2006

1996 Dodge Viper GTS

2001 Chevrolet revives two legendary labels, Z06 and LS6, for the latest, greatest Vette yet. The 2001 Z06 Corvette debuts with its new 5.7L LS6 small-block V8, an able challenger to its 454-cube LS6 forerunner of 1970 and '71.

1995 Last ZR-1 Corvette built. Dodge introduces its Viper GTS coupe as 1996 model. Ford's SVT Cobra-R appears with big 351-cid small-block and without backseat, radio or conditioning.

2002 New GT40 debuts at Detroit Auto Show. GM's F-body platform (Chevrolet's Camaro and Pontiac's Firebird) makes it final appearance. Mercury shows off its Mercury Marauder convertible concept car on the auto show circuit.

1998 Ford's four-door Taurus selected to replace Thunder-bird on NASCAR racing circuit.

2000 A third SVT Mustang Cobra-R appears, following in the tracks of race-ready Cobra-R models built for 1993 and 1995.

Above: Pontiac's GTO is reborn for 2004

Above: Chevrolet's Camaro SS was reborn in 1996

1996 SLP Engineering expands its reach into Chevrolet ranks, creating the new Camaro Z28 SS. Corvette gets optional LT4 V8 for one year only. Chevy's Impala SS discontinued.

1999 Pontiac marks 30 uninter-rupted years of Trans Am performance with a special-edition commemorative model sporting electric-blue wheels. Ford marks 35 years of Mustang tradition with barely discernible badges.

2003 Ford Motor Company celebrates is 100th anniversary, as does Buick. Mustang Mach 1 makes comeback. Chevrolet marks 50th birthday for "America's Sports Car," the Corvette. Mercury Marauder four-door debuts.

Left: A peek inside Chevrolet's 2001 Z06 Corvette.

1994 Ford's SVT Cobra Mustang convertible paces Indy 500. Chevrolet revives its Impala SS, this time basing it on a four-door Caprice platform.

1997 Chevrolet introduces all-new C5 Corvette, first as a coupe only. A convertible C5 follows the next year.

2004 The legend lives again as Pontiac unveils its new GTO. Both next-generation Mustang and new C6 Corvette unveiled.

Index

Acknowledgments

Mike Mueller for kindly waiving all his other deadlines to get this book done.
Phil Clucas for the amazing layouts.

Picture Credits

All photographs courtesy of Mike Mueller.